RUPA

Published by
Rupa Publications India Pvt. Ltd 2025
7/16, Ansari Road, Daryaganj
New Delhi 110002

Sales centres:
Bengaluru Chennai
Hyderabad Jaipur Kathmandu
Kolkata Mumbai Prayagraj

Photo Source: Wikimedia Commons

ISBN: 978-93-6156-268-6

First impression 2025

10 9 8 7 6 5 4 3 2 1

Printed in India

CONTENTS

SECTION FOUR
ADVANCED TECHNIQUES AND TRAINING

SECTION FIVE
NUTRITION, RECOVERY, AND MENTAL PREPARATION

SECTION SIX
COMPETITIVE GYMNASTICS

INTRODUCTION

GYMNASTICS IS A SPORT THAT EPITOMIZES THE fusion of strength, flexibility, agility, and grace. It's a discipline that pushes the boundaries of what the human body can achieve, requiring not just physical prowess but also a deep mental focus and resilience. Gymnastics demands a unique combination of power and finesse, where athletes must execute complex maneuvers with precision while maintaining an effortless elegance. Whether on the floor, beam, bars, or vault, each movement in gymnastics is a testament to the athlete's dedication and hours of practice.

At its core, gymnastics is about mastering control over one's body. The sport develops a keen sense of spatial awareness, balance, and coordination, which are essential for performing the various skills and routines that define the sport. From a young age, gymnasts learn to harness their energy and direct it with precision, whether they are flipping through the air or holding a handstand. The ability to combine explosive power with delicate balance is what sets gymnastics apart from other sports, making it both a physically demanding and visually captivating discipline.

Gymnastics is not just a sport; it's a journey of self-discovery and personal growth. It teaches athletes the importance of perseverance, discipline, and the pursuit of excellence. The challenges faced in training and competition mirror those in life, requiring gymnasts to develop a strong mindset and the ability to overcome obstacles.

One of the most compelling aspects of gymnastics is its diversity. The sport offers a wide range of disciplines, including artistic gymnastics, rhythmic gymnastics, trampoline, and tumbling, each with its unique set of skills and challenges. Artistic gymnastics, perhaps the most well-known, includes events like the floor exercise, balance beam, uneven bars, and vault, where athletes perform routines that combine acrobatics, dance, and strength elements. Rhythmic gymnastics emphasizes grace and coordination, with athletes performing routines with apparatus such as ribbons, hoops, and balls. Trampoline and tumbling focus on high-flying acrobatics and the execution of complex flips and twists in rapid succession.

The sport of gymnastics continues to evolve, with athletes pushing the limits of what is possible. New techniques and skills are constantly being developed, and the level of competition continues to rise. Gymnastics is a dynamic and ever-changing sport that captivates audiences with its blend of athleticism and artistry. It's a sport that inspires and challenges, offering a platform for athletes to showcase their strength, creativity, and dedication on a global stage.

1

THE HISTORY AND EVOLUTION OF GYMNASTICS

ORIGINS OF GYMNASTICS AS A SPORT

Gymnastics, one of the oldest forms of physical exercise, has roots that trace back to ancient civilizations, where the practice was integral to preparing individuals for battle and daily survival. The term "gymnastics" itself originates from the Greek word "gymnos," meaning "naked," which reflects the early practice of athletes training unclothed to achieve a pure focus on physical performance.

- **Ancient Greece:** In ancient Greece, gymnastics was more than just exercise; it was a way of life. The Greeks believed in the harmony of body and mind, and physical training was a crucial part of their education system. Gymnastics included a variety of physical activities such as running, jumping, and wrestling, which were seen as essential for developing a strong, capable, and disciplined individual. These activities were also closely tied to the Greek's religious and cultural practices, with athletes often participating in religious festivals and ceremonies.

Gymnastics and Rope Climbing (Greek)

- **Roman Influence:** The Roman Empire adopted and expanded upon Greek gymnastics, incorporating these practices into their military training. Roman soldiers were trained in various forms of gymnastics to enhance their strength, agility, and endurance, which were necessary for battle. However, after the fall of the Roman Empire, the practice of gymnastics saw a decline, becoming less prominent in society until its revival in the 18th and 19th centuries.

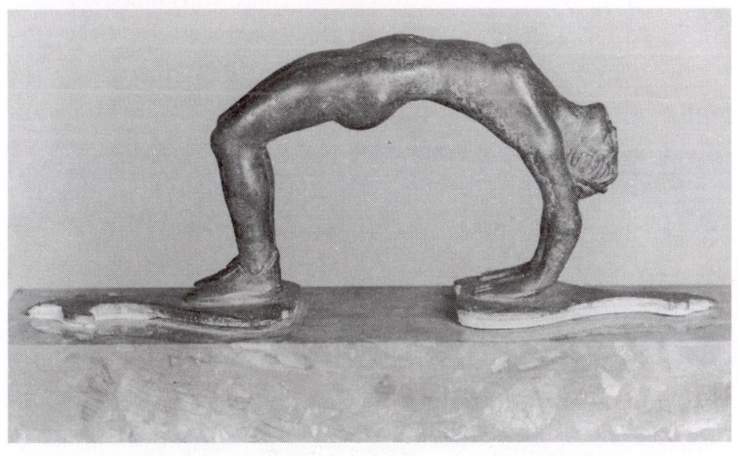

Praenestine–Cista Handle in the Form of a Woman Somersaulting, 5th Century BC (Roman)

DEVELOPMENT OF MODERN GYMNASTICS

The revival of gymnastics in the modern era began in the 19th century, largely due to the efforts of pioneers who recognized the importance of physical fitness in education and national pride.

Friedrich Ludwig Jahn and the Turnverein Movement:

The transformation of gymnastics into a structured and competitive sport can be credited to Friedrich Ludwig Jahn, known as the "Father of Modern Gymnastics." In the early 1800s, Jahn established the first gymnastics club in Germany, the Turnverein, which became the foundation of modern gymnastics. Jahn developed a system of exercises using equipment like the horizontal bar, parallel bars, and rings, which remain central to the sport today. His vision was to foster physical fitness as a means to strengthen the youth of Germany, both physically and morally, in the wake of the Napoleonic Wars.

Southside Turnverein, Indianapolis

Spread Across Europe and Beyond

Jahn's ideas quickly spread across Europe and to other parts of the world, influencing the development of gymnastics in countries like Sweden, France, and the United States. In Sweden, Per Henrik Ling developed a form of gymnastics focused on calisthenics and bodyweight exercises, emphasizing the health benefits of regular physical activity. Meanwhile, in the United States, the Turnverein movement took hold among German immigrants, leading to the establishment of gymnastics clubs across the country.

Friedrich Ludwig Jahn

Per Henrik Ling

Gymnastics in Education

By the late 19th and early 20th centuries, gymnastics had become an integral part of physical education in schools worldwide. Educators recognized the value of gymnastics in promoting physical health, discipline, and character development in young people. This period also saw the formalization of rules and the establishment of national and international competitions, setting the stage for gymnastics to become a globally recognized sport.

NOTABLE GYMNASTS AND MILESTONES

Gymnastics has a rich history of athletes who have left an indelible mark on the sport, pushing the boundaries of what is possible and inspiring generations of gymnasts to come.

Olympic Debut and Expansion

Gymnastics made its Olympic debut at the first modern Olympic Games in Athens in 1896, where it was one of the core sports. Initially, only men competed in the Games, with events focusing on apparatus exercises like the horizontal bar, parallel bars, and pommel horse. Women's gymnastics was introduced at the 1928 Amsterdam Olympics, and since then, the sport has expanded to include a wide range of events, including rhythmic gymnastics and trampoline, which were added to the Olympic program in the latter half of the 20th century.

Gymnastics at the 1896 Summer Olympics—Men's parallel bars

Women Gymnasts from 1928 Olympics

Pioneers and Legends

Throughout the 20th and 21st centuries, gymnastics has produced numerous iconic athletes who have become legends in the sport. Nadia Comăneci, a Romanian gymnast, became the first female gymnast to score a perfect 10 at the 1976 Montreal Olympics, setting a new standard for excellence in the sport. In more recent years, American gymnast Simone Biles has redefined the limits of human ability with her extraordinary performances, winning multiple Olympic gold medals and world championships. These athletes, among others, have not only advanced the technical aspects of

Nadia Comaneci

gymnastics but have also brought global attention and admiration to the sport.

Technical Innovations and Milestones

Over the decades, gymnastics has seen significant technical innovations that have pushed the sport forward. The development of new skills, such as the Yurchenko vault, named after Soviet gymnast Natalia Yurchenko, and the Biles, a move named after Simone Biles, which involves a double-twisting double backflip, have challenged and inspired gymnasts to continually raise the bar. Each generation of gymnasts has built upon the achievements of their predecessors, setting new records and breaking old ones, making gymnastics one of the most dynamic and evolving sports in the world.

Simone Biles

THE ROLE OF GYMNASTICS IN GLOBAL SPORTS

Gymnastics plays a vital role in the global sports community, not only as a competitive sport but also as a foundation for physical development and a tool for personal growth.

Gymnastics as a Foundation for Other Sports

Gymnastics is often seen as a foundational sport because it develops core strength, flexibility, balance, and coordination—skills that are crucial for success in almost any physical activity. Many athletes from other sports, such as diving, figure skating, and even football, use gymnastics training to improve their performance. The discipline and physical conditioning required in gymnastics also help athletes excel in other areas of their lives, making it a valuable component of any athletic training program.

Global Impact and Cultural Significance

Gymnastics has a significant cultural impact worldwide, promoting values such as discipline, perseverance, and resilience. It is a sport that is practiced by millions of people, from children in beginner classes to elite athletes competing on the world stage. Gymnastics clubs and schools provide a sense of community and belonging, where athletes support and motivate each other to reach their full potential.

The Future of Gymnastics

As gymnastics continues to grow in popularity, the sport is likely to see further innovations in training techniques, technology, and competition formats. The increasing use of technology, such as video analysis and biomechanical feedback, is helping athletes refine their techniques and improve performance. Additionally, as gymnastics becomes more globalized, with athletes from diverse backgrounds rising to prominence, the sport is poised to continue its evolution, inspiring future generations of gymnasts and fans alike.

SECTION ONE

GETTING STARTED

2

UNDERSTANDING GYMNASTICS AS A SPORT

GYMNASTICS IS A DYNAMIC AND MULTIFACETED sport that tests strength, flexibility, coordination, balance, and control. It involves performing exercises that challenge the body's physical limits while demanding precision and grace. At its core, gymnastics is about the mastery of movement, whether on the floor, the apparatus, or in the air. This sport is not only about physical prowess but also about mental discipline, as gymnasts must maintain focus and poise under intense pressure.

Gymnastics is distinguished by its versatility, offering a range of disciplines that cater to different interests and abilities. From the explosive power required in vaulting to the delicate control needed for balance beam routines, gymnastics covers a broad spectrum of athletic skills. Whether practiced recreationally or at a competitive level, gymnastics provides a comprehensive workout for the entire body, making it one of the most complete sports in terms of physical development.

TYPES OF GYMNASTICS: ARTISTIC, RHYTHMIC, TRAMPOLINE, AND MORE

Gymnastics is not a monolithic sport; it includes several distinct disciplines, each with its unique characteristics and challenges:

1. **Artistic Gymnastics:** The most widely recognized form, artistic gymnastics is divided into men's and women's events. Men's events include floor exercise, pommel horse, still rings, vault, parallel bars, and horizontal bar. Women's events consist of vault, uneven bars, balance beam, and floor exercise. This discipline emphasizes strength, flexibility, and acrobatics.

Artistic Gymnastics

2. **Rhythmic Gymnastics:** This form of gymnastics combines elements of ballet, dance, and apparatus manipulation (such as ribbons, hoops, balls, clubs, and ropes). Rhythmic gymnastics is performed exclusively by women and is known for its elegance and fluidity. The routines are choreographed to music, creating a graceful and expressive performance.

Rhythmic Gymnastics

3. **Trampoline Gymnastics:** This discipline focuses on aerial skills performed on a trampoline. Athletes execute a series of jumps, flips, and twists, reaching impressive heights while maintaining control and precision. Trampoline gymnastics is both a competitive sport and a training tool for other gymnastics disciplines.

Trampoline Gymnastics

4. **Acrobatic Gymnastics:** In this discipline, gymnasts work in pairs or groups to perform routines that combine acrobatic skills, dance, and tumbling. The routines involve lifts, throws, and catches, requiring exceptional teamwork, timing, and trust between partners.

Acrobatic Gymnastics

5. **Aerobic Gymnastics:** Known for its high-energy routines, aerobic gymnastics is characterized by continuous movement patterns set to upbeat music. It emphasizes strength, flexibility, and cardiovascular endurance, with routines that are fast-paced and demanding.

Aerobic Gymnastics

6. **Gymnastics for All:** Also known as general gymnastics, this discipline is inclusive and non-competitive, focusing on group performances that emphasize fun, fitness, and creativity. It is suitable for participants of all ages and abilities.

General Gymnastics

BASIC RULES AND REGULATIONS OF GYMNASTICS

The rules and regulations in gymnastics are designed to ensure fairness, safety, and standardization across competitions. Each gymnastics discipline has its own set of rules, governed by international bodies such as the International Gymnastics Federation (FIG). Key aspects include:

- **Scoring:** Gymnasts are judged based on the difficulty and execution of their routines. The final score is a combination of the difficulty score (which reflects the

complexity of the skills performed) and the execution score (which assesses the quality of the performance, including form, technique, and artistry). Deductions are made for errors such as falls, steps, or poor form.

- **Apparatus Specifications:** Each apparatus in gymnastics has specific dimensions and characteristics that must be adhered to in competitions. These standards ensure consistency and safety for the athletes.
- **Age and Eligibility:** Gymnasts must meet certain age and eligibility requirements to compete at various levels. For example, elite gymnasts typically start competing at a young age and must qualify through various stages to reach the highest levels of competition, such as the Olympics.
- **Routine Composition:** Gymnasts are required to perform a set of skills that meet certain criteria, including elements of difficulty, variety, and originality. The composition of the routine is crucial in maximizing the difficulty score while minimizing the risk of deductions.

OVERVIEW OF DIFFERENT GYMNASTICS EVENTS

Gymnastics competitions are structured around various events, each highlighting different aspects of the sport. In artistic gymnastics, for example:

- **Men's Events:**
    - *Floor Exercise*: Performed on a spring floor, this event showcases tumbling passes combined with strength and balance elements.

Floor Exercise (men)

- *Pommel Horse*: Focuses on circular movements and requires exceptional upper body strength and coordination.

Pommel Horse

- *Still Rings*: Emphasizes strength and control, with gymnasts performing static holds and dynamic moves on suspended rings.

Still Rings

- *Vault*: Involves sprinting towards a vaulting table and performing aerial maneuvers before landing.

Vault (men)

- *Parallel Bars*: Gymnasts perform swings, balances, and releases on two parallel bars.

Parallel Bars (men)

- *Horizontal Bar*: Features high-flying release moves and complex swing elements on a single bar.

Horizontal Bar (men)

- **Women's Events:**
  - *Vault*: Similar to the men's event, with a focus on explosive power and precision.

Vault (women)

  - *Uneven Bars:* Involves transitions between two bars at different heights, showcasing swinging and release skills.

Uneven Bars

- *Balance Beam*: A test of balance, poise, and nerve, as gymnasts perform acrobatic skills on a narrow beam.

Balance Beam

- *Floor Exercise*: Combines tumbling, dance, and acrobatics performed to music, highlighting the gymnast's expressiveness and athleticism.

Floor Exercise (women)

Each event requires a unique set of skills and contributes to the overall versatility of a gymnast. Mastery in these events comes from years of dedication, practice, and refinement, making gymnastics one of the most challenging and rewarding sports.

3

ESSENTIAL GEAR AND EQUIPMENT

GYMNASTICS IS A SPORT THAT BLENDS ARTISTRY, strength, precision, and athleticism. It requires athletes to perform complex movements on various apparatuses, and the right gear and equipment play a vital role in both enhancing performance and ensuring safety. This chapter delves into the essential gear every gymnast needs, from leotards to specialized equipment like grips and beams, and provides detailed guidance on caring for your gear to maintain peak performance.

LEOTARDS: COMPETITIVE VS. RECREATIONAL

Leotards are iconic in gymnastics, known for their sleek design and functional purpose. They are more than just a uniform; they are a critical part of a gymnast's performance attire, designed to offer support, flexibility, and style.

- **Competitive Leotards:** These leotards are engineered with high-performance materials such as Lycra, spandex, and nylon blends. They provide a snug fit that enhances movement while minimizing the risk of wardrobe malfunctions during routines. Competitive leotards are often embellished with rhinestones, sequins, and unique designs that make a visual impact during competitions. The fabric used is usually moisture-wicking and durable, capable of withstanding intense training sessions and the physical demands of competitive events. Moreover, competitive leotards are tailored to meet specific regulations set by governing bodies, such as ensuring proper coverage and avoiding distractions.

Competitive Leotard

- *Design Considerations*: The design of competitive leotards is often influenced by the gymnast's personal style and the team's colors. Customization is common, with many gymnasts opting for personalized leotards that reflect their personality or team spirit. The fit is meticulously crafted to allow for the full range of motion required in routines, from splits and flips to balance poses.
- *Material and Durability*: The materials used in competitive leotards are chosen for their durability and comfort. High-stretch fabrics allow for maximum flexibility, while advanced stitching techniques ensure that the leotard can endure the repetitive strains of practice and competition.

- **Recreational Leotards:** Designed for comfort and ease of movement, recreational leotards are perfect for training sessions and casual practice. These leotards are typically made from softer, more breathable fabrics like cotton blends or simple Lycra. They are less ornate than competitive leotards, focusing more on functionality than aesthetics.

Recreational Leotard

  - *Comfort and Fit*: Recreational leotards are designed with the comfort of the gymnast in mind. They offer a relaxed fit compared to their competitive counterparts, which makes them ideal for long training sessions where comfort is paramount.
  - *Cost and Accessibility*: Recreational leotards are

generally more affordable and widely available, making them accessible to gymnasts at all levels. They come in a variety of colors and patterns, offering gymnasts the opportunity to express their individuality even during practice.

GRIPS, CHALK, AND OTHER ACCESSORIES

In gymnastics, the hands and wrists are subjected to intense pressure, especially during events like bars and rings. The right accessories, such as grips and chalk, are essential for protecting these areas and enhancing performance.

- **Grips:** Gymnasts use grips to protect their hands and improve their grip on apparatuses like the uneven bars, high bar, and rings. Grips are made of durable leather and feature wrist straps that secure them in place. There are different types of grips tailored to specific events, such as dowel grips for bar routines, which provide additional grip strength and prevent slipping.
    - *Types of Grips*: There are several types of grips used in gymnastics, including palm grips, dowel grips, and beginner grips. Each type serves a specific purpose:
        - *Palm Grips:* Commonly used by beginners, palm grips cover the palm and provide basic protection and grip.
        - *Dowel Grips:* Used by advanced gymnasts, these grips feature a dowel rod that fits into the fingers, offering superior grip strength on bars.

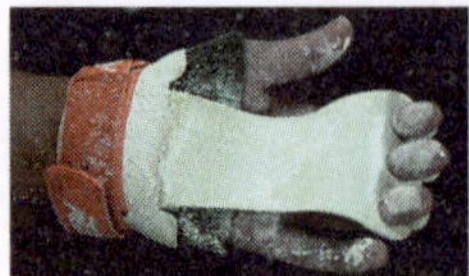
Palm Grip

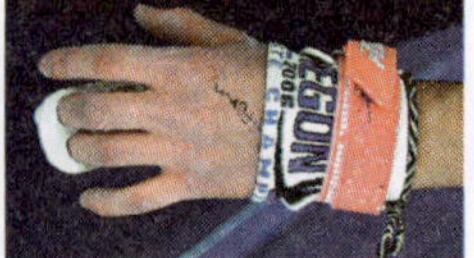
Dowel Grip

Velcro Grip

        - *Buckles vs. Velcro:* Grips are secured with either buckle or Velcro straps. Buckle grips offer a more secure fit, while Velcro grips are easier to adjust.
    - *Maintenance and Replacement:* Regular inspection of grips is necessary to prevent accidents. Worn-out grips should be replaced immediately to avoid slips and injuries. It's also important to break in new grips gradually to prevent discomfort or blisters.
- **Chalk:** Magnesium carbonate, or gym chalk, is a staple in gymnastics. It is applied to the hands and feet to absorb moisture and improve grip, especially on bars and rings. Chalk is also used on apparatuses to reduce slipping and enhance control during routines.

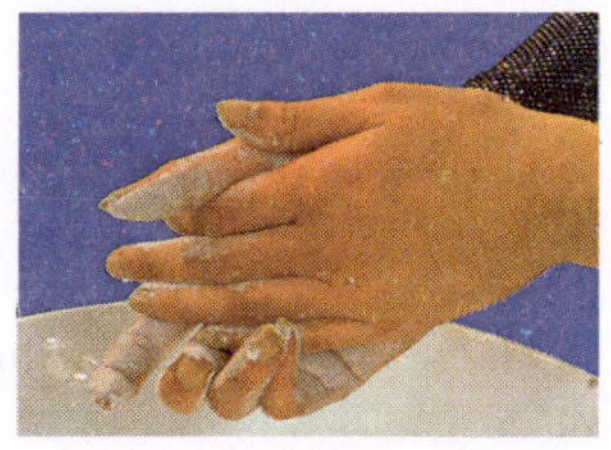
Chalk

    - *Application Techniques*: Proper application of chalk involves dusting the hands and apparatus lightly to avoid excess buildup, which can cause slippery

conditions. Some gymnasts prefer liquid chalk, which is less messy and provides a consistent layer of grip.

- *Chalk Bags and Storage*: Chalk should be stored in a dry, airtight container to maintain its effectiveness. Many gymnasts carry personal chalk bags to ensure they have a reliable supply during practice and competitions.

- **Wrist Supports and Guards:** Given the high-impact nature of gymnastics, wrist supports and guards are critical for injury prevention. These accessories help stabilize the wrists, reducing the risk of sprains, strains, and overuse injuries.
  - *Wrist Guards*: Commonly used during vaults and tumbling, wrist guards provide extra padding and support, helping to absorb the shock from landings and flips. They are particularly useful for gymnasts with a history of wrist injuries or those performing high-impact skills.
  - *Wrist Straps*: These are essential for events like rings and bars, where the wrists endure significant strain. Wrist straps help secure grips and provide additional support, ensuring the gymnast can maintain control throughout their routine.
- **Footwear:** While gymnastics is typically performed barefoot to enhance grip and control, some events or training sessions may require specialized footwear.
  - *Beam Shoes*: These lightweight shoes offer additional grip on the balance beam, helping gymnasts maintain stability during complex routines. They are designed to fit snugly, allowing the gymnast to feel the apparatus while providing extra traction.

Beam Shoes

Toe Shoes

- *Toe Shoes*: These are sometimes worn during floor exercises to provide a bit more support without sacrificing the feel of the floor. They are particularly beneficial for gymnasts with foot injuries or those requiring extra arch support.

UNDERSTANDING GYM EQUIPMENT: BEAMS, BARS, MATS, ETC.

The equipment used in gymnastics is diverse and specialized, each piece playing a critical role in training and performance. Mastery of this equipment is essential for success in the sport.

- **Balance Beam:** One of the most challenging apparatuses in women's gymnastics, the balance beam requires immense concentration, precision, and balance. The beam is 10 centimeters wide and 5 meters long, elevated to 1.2 meters above the ground.

Balance Beam Training

- *Training Techniques*: Gymnasts often begin training on low beams before progressing to the standard height. Drills for beam routines focus on developing balance, coordination, and the ability to perform complex skills under pressure.
- *Safety Measures*: Mats are placed around the beam to cushion falls, and coaches often spot gymnasts during difficult maneuvers. Regular checks of the beam's surface for wear and tear are crucial to ensure safety.

- **Uneven Bars:** Used in women's artistic gymnastics, the uneven bars consist of two horizontal bars set at different heights. Routines on the uneven bars require gymnasts to swing, transition, and release between the bars, demonstrating strength, flexibility, and timing.

Uneven Bars Training

  - *Bar Settings*: The distance between the bars is adjustable to accommodate gymnasts of different sizes and preferences. This flexibility allows gymnasts to perform routines that best suit their body mechanics.
  - *Training Focus*: Training on the uneven bars emphasizes grip strength, upper body power, and the ability to execute precise transitions. Coaches work with gymnasts to develop fluidity in their movements and maintain momentum throughout the routine.

- **Parallel Bars:** A key apparatus in men's artistic gymnastics, the parallel bars require strength, control, and coordination. Gymnasts perform a variety of swings, balances, and dismounts, utilizing both their upper and lower body.

Parallel Bars

- *Techniques and Skills*: Mastery of the parallel bars involves developing core strength and the ability to control movements between static holds and dynamic swings. Training often includes specific drills to improve balance and the smooth transition between elements.
- *Apparatus Maintenance*: Ensuring that the bars are secure and properly spaced is essential for safety. Regular inspection and maintenance are necessary to prevent accidents during practice and competitions.

- **Horizontal Bar:** Also known as the high bar, this apparatus is used in men's artistic gymnastics and demands exceptional upper body strength and timing. Gymnasts perform continuous swings and high-flying release moves before executing a controlled landing.

Horizontal Bar Training

- *Focus Areas*: Training on the horizontal bar emphasizes grip strength, endurance, and the ability to perform aerial maneuvers with precision. The high bar is also where gymnasts develop their dismount skills, which are critical for scoring.
- *Safety Practices*: Mats are strategically placed under the high bar to cushion landings, and spotters are often used during practice to prevent injuries from falls.

- **Vaulting Table:** The vault is a dynamic event where gymnasts sprint towards a springboard, propel themselves off the vaulting table, and execute flips and twists in the air before landing. The vaulting table is designed to provide the necessary rebound and support for these explosive movements.
  - *Training and Technique*: Successful vaulting requires speed, power, and precise technique. Gymnasts practice their run-up, springboard takeoff, and vault execution to ensure they can achieve the desired height and rotation. Drills often include the use of

a foam pit or crash mat to practice the landing and transition smoothly from the vault to the mat.

Vaulting Table

- *Safety Considerations*: The vaulting table is equipped with padding to reduce the impact on falls, and coaches use spotting techniques to assist gymnasts during training. Ensuring that the table is correctly adjusted to the appropriate height for each gymnast is crucial for both safety and performance.

- **Floor Exercise:** The floor exercise is a routine performed on a 12x12 meter mat that combines tumbling passes, dance elements, and acrobatics. It is an event that allows gymnasts to showcase their flexibility, strength, and creativity.
  - *Routine Composition*: Floor routines are choreographed to music and include a series of tumbling passes, jumps, and dance movements. Gymnasts are judged on their execution, artistry, and the difficulty of the skills performed.

Floor Exercise–Acrobatics

- *Training Tips*: Effective floor training involves building strength and flexibility, practicing choreography, and ensuring clean, precise execution of tumbling passes. Coaches focus on improving fluidity, rhythm, and the ability to perform under the pressure of competition.

- **Mats and Safety Equipment:** Mats are used across various gymnastics apparatuses to provide cushioning and minimize the risk of injury. They come in various sizes and types, such as landing mats, practice mats, and safety mats.
  - *Types of Mats*:
    - *Landing Mats:* Thick and designed to absorb impact from high falls or dismounts. They are often used under the high bar, vault, and uneven bars.
    - *Practice Mats:* Thicker and softer than competition mats, practice mats are used during training to provide additional safety and comfort.

Landing Mat

Practice Mat

- *Safety Mats:* Smaller mats used around apparatuses to catch gymnasts who may fall or slip during practice.

- *Maintenance*: Regular inspection of mats for wear and tear is important to ensure their effectiveness. Mats should be kept clean and dry to prevent slipping and maintain their cushioning properties.

Safety Mat

CARING FOR YOUR GEAR

Proper maintenance of gymnastics gear is essential for ensuring safety, extending the lifespan of the equipment, and maintaining peak performance. Here are some key practices for caring for your gymnastics gear:

- **Leotards:**
  - *Washing*: Leotards should be washed after each use to remove sweat and bacteria. Use a gentle detergent and cold water to prevent damage to the fabric. Avoid wringing out the leotard, as this can distort its shape.
  - *Drying*: Air-dry leotards by laying them flat on a clean towel. Avoid using a dryer, as the heat can damage the elastic fibers. Store leotards in a cool, dry place to prevent mildew growth.

- **Grips:**
  - *Cleaning*: Wipe grips with a damp cloth after each use to remove chalk residue and sweat. Avoid soaking grips, as this can weaken the leather.
  - *Storage*: Store grips in a dry place to prevent mold and deterioration. Use a breathable bag or pouch to keep them clean and protected from dust and debris.
- **Chalk:**
  - *Handling*: Store chalk in an airtight container to keep it dry and effective. Keep the chalk bag or container clean to avoid contamination.
  - *Usage*: Apply chalk sparingly to avoid excess buildup, which can create a slippery surface. Clean up any spilled chalk promptly to maintain a safe training environment.
- **Gym Equipment:**
  - *Routine Checks*: Regularly inspect gym equipment for signs of wear and tear. Ensure that apparatuses are securely anchored and free of damage.
  - *Cleaning*: Wipe down equipment with a clean, damp cloth to remove sweat and chalk. For thorough cleaning, use appropriate disinfectants to maintain hygiene and prevent the spread of germs.
  - *Repairs*: Address any repairs or maintenance issues promptly. Consult with a professional technician for complex repairs to ensure that the equipment remains safe and functional.

By understanding the essential gear and equipment used in gymnastics and following proper maintenance practices, gymnasts can enhance their performance and ensure a safe and enjoyable training experience.

4

THE BASICS OF GYM SAFETY

GYMNASTICS, WHILE EXHILARATING AND rewarding, demands a high level of safety awareness due to its physically demanding nature. Understanding the basics of gym safety is essential for preventing injuries and ensuring a positive training environment. This chapter delves into key aspects of gym safety, including understanding risks, effective spotting, the role of coaches, and responding to injuries.

UNDERSTANDING GYM SAFETY: RISKS AND PRECAUTIONS

Gymnastics involves complex movements and high-impact activities, which inherently carry some risk of injury. Recognizing these risks and taking appropriate precautions is crucial for minimizing accidents.

- **Common Risks:**
    - *Falls and Slips*: Gymnasts often perform high-flying stunts and landings that can result in falls. Proper

matting and equipment can help mitigate these risks.

- *Overuse Injuries*: Repetitive strain from performing the same movements can lead to overuse injuries, such as tendinitis or stress fractures.
- *Equipment-Related Injuries*: Improper use of gymnastics apparatus or faulty equipment can lead to injuries.

- **Precautions:**
  - *Proper Equipment*: Ensure all gym equipment is well-maintained and in good working order. Use appropriate mats and padding to absorb impacts.
  - *Warm-Up and Stretching*: Always perform a thorough warm-up and stretching routine before engaging in gymnastics to prepare the body and reduce the risk of strains and sprains.
  - *Technique and Form*: Focus on learning and practicing correct techniques to avoid unnecessary stress on the body and reduce the risk of injury.

SPOTTING AND SAFETY MEASURES

Spotting is an essential safety technique used in gymnastics to assist gymnasts during complex maneuvers. Proper spotting not only helps prevent falls but also builds confidence in performing difficult skills.

- **Effective Spotting Techniques:**
  - *Positioning*: Spotters should position themselves close to the gymnast, ensuring they can intervene quickly if necessary. For skills involving rotation or

flips, spotters often place themselves in a position where they can help guide the gymnast through the skill.

- *Communication*: Clear communication between the gymnast and spotter is crucial. Spotters should discuss the intended skill and any potential concerns before practice begins.
- *Supportive Contact*: Spotters should use appropriate contact to support the gymnast without taking over the movement. This includes supporting the gymnast's body weight during lifts or falls while allowing them to practice their technique.

- **Safety Measures:**
  - *Safety Mats and Padding*: Ensure that all apparatuses are equipped with adequate padding and that mats are placed correctly under equipment and landing areas.
  - *Safe Environment*: Keep the gym area free from obstacles and hazards. Ensure that the floor and equipment are clean and dry to prevent slips and falls.

THE ROLE OF COACHES AND TRAINERS

Coaches and trainers play a pivotal role in maintaining gym safety. Their responsibilities extend beyond teaching skills and include fostering a safe and supportive training environment.

- **Role of Coaches:**
  - *Skill Development*: Coaches should focus on teaching correct techniques and progressions to ensure

gymnasts perform skills safely. They must also monitor each gymnast's form and make adjustments as needed.
    - *Safety Protocols*: Coaches are responsible for implementing and enforcing safety protocols. This includes ensuring that gymnasts use equipment properly and adhere to safety guidelines.
    - *Emergency Preparedness*: Coaches should be trained in first aid and CPR. They must also be familiar with emergency procedures and how to respond to injuries or accidents.
- **Role of Trainers:**
    - *Conditioning and Strengthening*: Trainers help gymnasts build strength and flexibility, which are essential for injury prevention. They design conditioning programs tailored to the needs of the gymnast.
    - *Injury Prevention*: Trainers work closely with gymnasts to identify and address potential injury risks through targeted exercises and proper technique.
    - *Rehabilitation*: In the event of an injury, trainers assist with rehabilitation and recovery, ensuring that gymnasts return to training safely and effectively.

HOW TO RESPOND TO GYM INJURIES

Despite best efforts, injuries can occur in gymnastics. Knowing how to respond promptly and effectively is crucial for minimizing the impact of an injury and ensuring proper recovery.

- **Immediate Response:**
  - *Assessment*: Quickly assess the injured area and the severity of the injury. Look for signs of swelling, bruising, or severe pain.
  - *First Aid*: Apply first aid as necessary. For minor injuries, such as strains or sprains, use the R.I.C.E. method (Rest, Ice, Compression, Elevation). For more severe injuries, such as fractures or head injuries, seek immediate medical attention.
- **Seeking Medical Attention:**
  - *When to Seek Help*: If the injury is severe, persistent, or accompanied by symptoms like intense pain, inability to move the affected area, or numbness, seek medical attention promptly.
  - *Follow-Up Care*: Follow the recommendations of healthcare professionals for treatment and rehabilitation. Adhere to any prescribed rest and recovery protocols to ensure a full recovery.
- **Returning to Training:**
  - *Gradual Return*: Gradually ease back into training based on guidance from medical professionals. Start with light exercises and slowly progress to more intense activities.
  - *Monitoring*: Pay close attention to any lingering discomfort or pain. Report any issues to your coach or trainer to adjust the training plan as needed.

By understanding and implementing these safety practices, gymnasts, coaches, and trainers can work together to create a safe and effective training environment, minimizing the risk of injuries and ensuring that everyone can enjoy the sport to its fullest.

SECTION TWO

LEARNING THE FUNDAMENTALS

5

GETTING COMFORTABLE IN THE GYM

NAVIGATING THE WORLD OF GYMNASTICS INVOLVES more than mastering techniques and routines. It requires building confidence, overcoming fears, and becoming familiar with the equipment and apparatuses. This chapter focuses on helping gymnasts, whether beginners or those looking to refine their skills, become comfortable in the gym through overcoming fear, learning basic techniques, and developing confidence on various apparatuses.

OVERCOMING FEAR OF EQUIPMENT

Gymnastics equipment, with its varied shapes, heights, and functionalities, can be intimidating, especially for newcomers. Overcoming this fear is essential for progressing and enjoying the sport.

- **Gradual Exposure:**
    - *Familiarization*: Start by familiarizing yourself with the equipment from a safe distance. Understand its purpose and how it's used.

- *Low Heights and Soft Surfaces*: Begin with equipment at lower heights or use softer surfaces like mats to reduce the risk of injury. Gradually increase the height and complexity as comfort grows.
- *Controlled Environments*: Practice in a controlled environment with supervision. Use spotting and safety equipment to build confidence before attempting more advanced skills.

- **Mental Preparation:**
  - *Visualization*: Visualize successfully performing skills on the equipment. This mental practice can help reduce anxiety and build confidence.
  - *Positive Reinforcement*: Celebrate small successes and improvements. Positive reinforcement can help shift focus from fear to accomplishment.
- **Support and Encouragement:**
  - *Coaching Guidance*: Work with a coach or trainer who can provide guidance, encouragement, and reassurance. Their experience can help ease fears and build confidence.
  - *Peer Support*: Engage with fellow gymnasts who can offer support and share their own experiences. Being part of a supportive community can help alleviate fears.

BASIC TUMBLING TECHNIQUES

Tumbling is a fundamental aspect of gymnastics that involves a series of acrobatic movements performed on the floor. Mastering basic tumbling techniques is essential for developing more advanced skills.

- **Forward Roll:**
    - *Execution*: Start from a standing position, tuck your chin to your chest, and roll forward along your back. Use your arms to push off the floor and maintain momentum.
    - *Practice Tips*: Practice on a soft surface or mat. Focus on keeping your body tight and rolling smoothly without letting your head touch the floor.

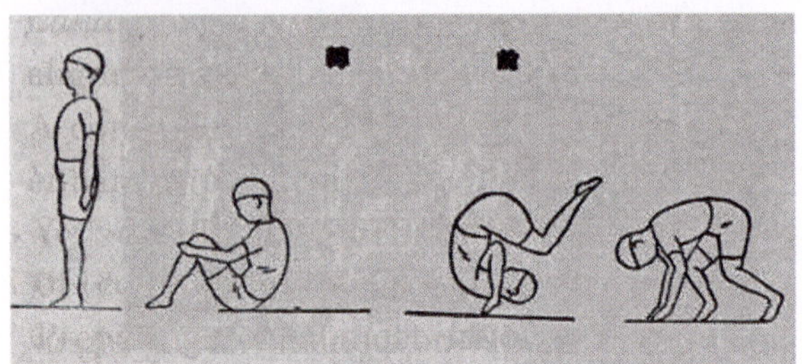

Forward Roll

- **Back Roll (Perform the same steps as a forward roll, but do them in reverse):**
    - *Execution*: Start from a sitting position, tuck your chin to your chest, and roll backward along your back. Push off with your feet to gain momentum.
    - *Practice Tips*: Ensure you have a spotter if needed. Use a mat for added safety and practice rolling in a straight line.
- **Cartwheel:**
    - *Execution*: Begin in a standing position, kick one leg up and over, and follow with the other leg while placing your hands on the floor. Land back on your feet.

  - *Practice Tips*: Focus on keeping your body straight and your movements controlled. Practice against a wall or with a spotter to build confidence.

Cartwheel

- **Handstand:**
  - *Execution*: Start from a standing position, kick your legs up and over, and balance on your hands. Keep your body straight and engage your core.
  - *Practice Tips*: Use a wall for support initially. Practice kicking up with control and holding the position for a few seconds.

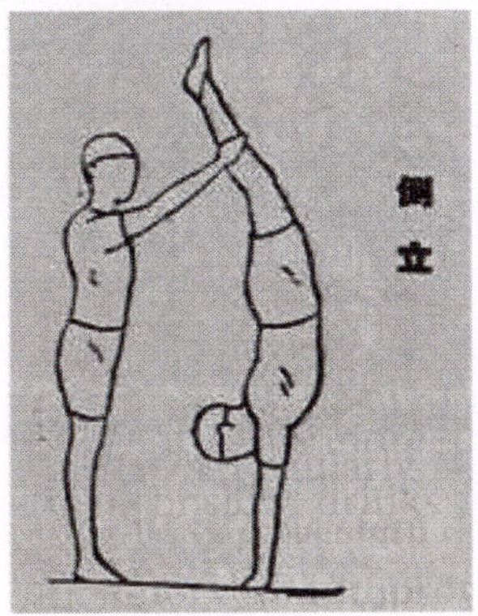

Handstand

STRETCHING AND FLEXIBILITY ROUTINES

Flexibility is crucial in gymnastics, as it enhances performance, prevents injuries, and aids in mastering various skills. Incorporating regular stretching into your routine can improve overall flexibility.

- **Dynamic Stretching:**
    - *Leg Swings*: Stand on one leg and swing the other leg forward and backward. This helps loosen up the hip flexors and hamstrings.

Leg Swing

Arm Circles

-
    - *Arm Circles*: Extend your arms to the sides and make small circles, gradually increasing in size. This warms up the shoulders and upper back.
- **Static Stretching:**
    - *Hamstring Stretch*: Sit on the floor with one leg extended and reach towards your toes. Hold the stretch to improve hamstring flexibility.

Hamstring Stretch

Quadriceps Stretch

  - *Quadriceps Stretch*: Stand on one leg, pull the other leg towards your buttocks, and hold. This stretches the front of the thigh.
  - *Hip Flexor Stretch*: Kneel on one knee with the other foot in front. Push your hips forward to stretch the hip flexors.

Hip Flexor Stretch

- **Flexibility Routines:**
  - *Daily Stretching*: Incorporate stretching into your daily routine. Focus on major muscle groups used in gymnastics, such as the hamstrings, quadriceps, and back.
  - *Routine Integration*: Include stretching as part of your warm-up and cool-down routines. This helps

maintain flexibility and prepares your body for intense training.

BUILDING CONFIDENCE ON DIFFERENT APPARATUS

Confidence on various gymnastics apparatuses, such as the beam, bars, and vault, is built through practice, proper technique, and positive reinforcement.

- **Beam:**
    - *Basic Skills*: Start with basic skills like walking and simple balances on the beam. Gradually progress to more complex skills as comfort increases.

Beam Balance Training

 - *Practice Tips*: Use a low beam or a padded surface initially. Focus on maintaining balance and correct posture.

- **Bars:**
    - *Basic Skills*: Practice basic skills such as swings and pulls on the bars. Work on grip strength and body control.
    - *Practice Tips*: Use spotting and safety equipment. Break down complex skills into smaller components and practice each part individually.

Swings on Bars

- **Vault:**
    - *Basic Skills*: Begin with basic vaulting drills, such as handsprings or simple jumps. Focus on technique and proper landing.
    - *Practice Tips:* Use a vaulting horse with padding or a soft surface. Gradually increase the height and complexity of the vault as confidence grows.

Vault Training

- **Parallel Bars and Pommel Horse:**
    - *Basic Skills*: Work on basic skills like swings and holds. Develop strength and coordination specific to each apparatus.
    - *Practice Tips*: Practice with appropriate spotting and safety measures. Focus on maintaining control and fluidity in movements.

Parallel Bars Training

Pommel Horse Training

By focusing on these fundamental aspects—overcoming fears, mastering basic techniques, maintaining flexibility, and building confidence—gymnasts can develop a strong foundation for their sport. These practices help ensure a safe and enjoyable gymnastics experience while laying the groundwork for more advanced skills and routines.

6

INTRODUCTION TO THE MAIN DISCIPLINES

GYMNASTICS IS A DIVERSE SPORT THAT encompasses several disciplines, each with its own unique demands and characteristics. These disciplines provide different avenues for athletes to showcase their skills, whether through artistic expression, rhythmic coordination, or aerial prowess. This chapter explores the main disciplines in gymnastics: Artistic Gymnastics, Rhythmic Gymnastics, and Trampoline and Tumbling, providing an overview of each to help enthusiasts and aspiring gymnasts understand their options and find their ideal fit.

OVERVIEW OF ARTISTIC GYMNASTICS

Artistic Gymnastics is the most widely recognized form of gymnastics, prominently featured in the Olympic Games and other international competitions. It involves performing routines on specific apparatuses, showcasing a blend of strength, flexibility, balance, and coordination.

- **Men's Artistic Gymnastics:**
  - *Floor Exercise*: This event involves a routine performed on a 12x12 meter mat, emphasizing tumbling, jumps, and acrobatics. Gymnasts aim for fluidity and power in their movements, combining strength with artistic presentation.
  - *Pommel Horse*: Gymnasts perform swings and rotations around a horse-shaped apparatus with handles. This event focuses on core strength and precision, requiring athletes to maintain balance while executing complex routines.
  - *Still Rings*: This event requires gymnasts to perform static holds and swinging movements on rings suspended from a high bar. It highlights upper body strength, stability, and control.
  - *Vault*: In this event, gymnasts sprint down a runway, launch off a vaulting horse, perform an aerial maneuver, and land on a mat. The vault combines speed, power, and precision.
  - *Parallel Bars*: Gymnasts perform a routine on two parallel bars, featuring swings, balances, and transitions. This event demands strength and coordination, focusing on fluid movement between the bars.
  - *Horizontal Bar*: This apparatus involves swinging and releasing maneuvers on a single high bar. Gymnasts showcase their strength and control through dynamic movements and catches.
- **Women's Artistic Gymnastics:**
  - *Floor Exercise*: Similar to the men's event but often incorporating more dance elements and

choreography. Routines are judged on artistic expression, difficulty, and execution.

- *Vault*: Includes a sprint down the runway, a vaulting maneuver, and a controlled landing. It emphasizes explosive power and precise technique.
- *Balance Beam*: Gymnasts perform a routine on a narrow beam, demonstrating balance, flexibility, and acrobatic skills. This event requires precision and composure, as athletes must perform intricate movements on a small surface.
- *Uneven Bars*: Involves swinging between two bars set at different heights. This event focuses on fluid transitions and a combination of strength and agility.

Artistic Gymnastics combines athleticism with artistic expression, making it suitable for individuals who enjoy performing complex routines and displaying both physical skill and grace.

RHYTHMIC GYMNASTICS: COMBINING DANCE AND GYMNASTICS

Rhythmic Gymnastics is a distinctive discipline that blends elements of dance with gymnastics, performed exclusively by women. It involves routines with hand-held apparatuses, emphasizing coordination, flexibility, and rhythm.

- **Apparatuses:**
  - *Rope*: Gymnasts perform tricks involving jumps, throws, and swings with a rope. This apparatus requires precise timing and control.

Gymnastics Using Rope

- *Hoop*: Routines include rolling, spinning, and tossing the hoop. The focus is on fluidity and creativity in using the hoop to complement dance movements.

Gymnastics Using Hoop

- *Ball*: Gymnasts use a ball to execute routines involving rolling, bouncing, and catching. The ball adds a dynamic element to the performance, requiring skillful manipulation.

Gymnastics Using Ball

- *Clubs*: Two clubs are used to perform routines that include swinging and twirling. This apparatus emphasizes coordination and synchronization.

Gymnastics Using Clubs

- *Ribbon*: A long ribbon attached to a stick is used to create patterns and movements. The ribbon's flow enhances the visual appeal of the routine.

Gymnastics Using Ribbon

- **Performance Elements:**
  - *Choreography*: Rhythmic Gymnastics routines are characterized by their choreographed dance elements, integrating gymnastic skills with artistic movements.
  - *Grace and Precision*: Routines are judged on the grace, precision, and fluidity of movements, as well as the effective use of apparatuses. Athletes must demonstrate a combination of technical skill and artistic flair.

Rhythmic Gymnastics requires a high level of artistry and coordination, making it ideal for those who enjoy performing choreographed routines that blend dance with gymnastic skills.

TRAMPOLINE AND TUMBLING: AERIAL SKILLS AND CONTROL

Trampoline and Tumbling focus on performing aerial skills and maintaining control during flight, offering a different perspective on gymnastics with an emphasis on explosive power and precision.

- **Trampoline:**
    - *Individual Trampoline*: Gymnasts perform a series of acrobatic skills and flips while bouncing on a trampoline. This event highlights height, control, and the ability to execute complex aerial maneuvers.

Individual Trampoline

    - *Synchronized Trampoline*: Pairs of gymnasts perform synchronized routines on individual trampolines. Coordination and harmony are key, with both athletes executing the same movements simultaneously.

Synchronized Trampoline

- **Tumbling:**
  - *Floor Tumbling*: Gymnasts perform acrobatic movements on a spring floor, including flips, twists, and somersaults. Tumbling routines focus on explosive power and precise landings.

Floor Tumbling

  - *Double Mini-Trampoline*: A smaller trampoline is used for routines that include jumps, flips, and landings. This event combines elements of trampoline and tumbling, emphasizing both height and control.

Double Mini Trampoline

Trampoline and Tumbling are well-suited for individuals who excel in aerial skills and enjoy the challenge of performing complex maneuvers with precision.

CHOOSING THE RIGHT DISCIPLINE FOR YOU

Selecting the right gymnastics discipline depends on individual interests, strengths, and goals. Consider the following factors:

- **Interests:** Reflect on what excites you about gymnastics. Whether it's performing artistic routines, blending dance with gymnastics, or mastering aerial skills, choose a discipline that aligns with your passions.
- **Strengths and Skills:** Evaluate your physical strengths and skills. Artistic Gymnastics requires a mix of strength and grace, Rhythmic Gymnastics emphasizes flexibility and coordination, and Trampoline and Tumbling focus on power and aerial control.
- **Goals:** Determine your goals within the sport. Whether aiming for competitive success, personal development, or simply enjoying the sport, choose a discipline that fits your aspirations.

Understanding the different gymnastics disciplines helps in making an informed decision about which path to pursue, allowing for a fulfilling and enjoyable experience in the sport.

SECTION THREE

MASTERING THE BASICS

7

FLOOR EXERCISE

THE FLOOR EXERCISE IS A DYNAMIC AND VISUALLY captivating component of gymnastics that combines tumbling, dance, and artistic expression. It is a showcase of both athletic prowess and creative performance. This chapter delves into the key aspects of the floor exercise, including the mechanics of floor tumbling, techniques for improving power and technique, choreography, and common mistakes with their corrections.

MECHANICS OF FLOOR TUMBLING

Floor tumbling involves a series of acrobatic movements performed on a spring floor, designed to highlight strength, agility, and control. Understanding the mechanics of these movements is crucial for executing them effectively.

- **Fundamentals of Tumbling:**
  - *Takeoff and Flight*: Tumbling begins with a powerful takeoff from the floor, utilizing a combination of

strength and momentum. Athletes must engage their core and leg muscles to achieve maximum height and control during flight.

  - *Body Positioning*: Proper body alignment is essential for maintaining balance and executing complex maneuvers. This includes keeping the body straight during aerial movements and achieving correct positioning for landings.
  - *Landing*: The landing phase requires precise control to absorb impact and maintain stability. Gymnasts should aim for a soft, controlled landing with knees slightly bent to reduce the risk of injury.

- **Key Tumbling Skills:**
  - *Front Handspring*: A forward movement where the gymnast places their hands on the floor while rotating their body. It is fundamental for linking other skills.
  - *Back Handspring*: A backward rotation performed on the hands, typically used as a transition between other skills or in combination with flips.
  - *Aerials and Flips*: These advanced skills involve rotating in the air without touching the floor. Mastery of these skills requires strength, technique, and practice.

IMPROVING POWER AND TECHNIQUE

Enhancing power and technique in floor exercise involves a combination of strength training, skill practice, and refining movement techniques.

- **Strength Training:**
  - *Core Strength*: A strong core is essential for maintaining balance and control during tumbling. Exercises such as planks, leg raises, and Russian twists can build core strength.
  - *Leg Power*: Powerful legs are necessary for explosive takeoffs and controlled landings. Plyometric exercises like box jumps, squats, and lunges can improve leg power.
  - *Upper Body Strength*: Strength in the arms and shoulders supports the execution of skills like handsprings and flips. Push-ups, pull-ups, and shoulder presses are effective for building upper body strength.
- **Technique Refinement:**
  - *Drills and Repetitions*: Regular practice of specific tumbling drills helps in refining technique. Repetitive practice of basic skills ensures muscle memory and precision.
  - *Feedback and Coaching*: Working with a coach to receive feedback and correct form is invaluable. Coaches can provide insights into technique adjustments and offer guidance on improving performance.
- **Flexibility and Conditioning:**
  - *Stretching Routines*: Incorporating flexibility training into your routine enhances the range of motion and reduces the risk of injury. Dynamic stretching before workouts and static stretching after can improve flexibility.
  - *Conditioning Exercises*: Regular conditioning

helps in building endurance and maintaining peak physical fitness. Incorporate exercises that mimic the demands of floor exercise to prepare the body for performance.

CHOREOGRAPHY AND ARTISTIC EXPRESSION

Floor exercise is not only about technical proficiency but also about artistic expression and choreography. Crafting a captivating routine involves blending technical skills with creative elements.

- **Routine Composition:**
    - *Music Selection*: Choose music that complements the routine and enhances the performance. The music should align with the tempo and mood of the routine, helping to convey the desired artistic expression.
    - *Choreography*: Design a routine that incorporates a variety of skills and transitions. The choreography should flow smoothly, with seamless connections between tumbling passes and dance elements.
    - *Artistic Presentation*: Emphasize grace, poise, and expression throughout the routine. Artistic presentation is judged on the ability to engage the audience and convey emotion through movement.
- **Performance Elements:**
    - *Facial Expressions*: Express emotions and engage the audience with facial expressions. Conveying confidence and enjoyment adds to the overall performance quality.
    - *Body Language*: Utilize body language to enhance

the performance, including dynamic movements and expressive gestures that align with the music and choreography.

COMMON MISTAKES AND CORRECTIONS

Understanding common mistakes in floor exercise and their corrections helps in improving performance and avoiding injuries.

- **Mistakes and Corrections:**
  - *Lack of Height in Jumps*: Insufficient height during jumps can affect the execution of skills. Focus on explosive leg power and proper technique to achieve greater height.
  - *Poor Body Alignment*: Misalignment can lead to balance issues and poor execution. Ensure proper body positioning during takeoffs, flight, and landings through consistent practice and feedback.
  - *Inconsistent Landings*: Difficulty in landing smoothly can impact overall performance. Practice landing drills and focus on absorbing impact with control to achieve stable landings.

By focusing on these key aspects—mechanics, power, technique, choreography, and common mistakes—gymnasts can develop a strong foundation in floor exercise, enhance their performance, and achieve their full potential in this dynamic and artistic discipline.

8

BALANCE BEAM

THE BALANCE BEAM IS A QUINTESSENTIAL APPARATUS in gymnastics, combining precision, grace, and daring. As one of the most challenging events, it demands a high level of balance, strength, and technique. This chapter delves into the intricacies of balance beam work, including the mechanics of beam routines, foot placement, body control, balancing techniques, creativity, and common mistakes with their corrections.

MECHANICS OF BEAM WORK

The balance beam is a narrow, elevated apparatus that tests a gymnast's ability to maintain balance while performing complex routines. Understanding the mechanics of beam work is crucial for mastering this discipline.

- **The Beam:**
    - *Dimensions*: The balance beam is 4 meters long, 10 centimeters wide, and 1.2 meters off the ground.

These dimensions create a challenging platform for performing intricate skills.

  - *Surface*: The beam's surface is covered with a padded, synthetic material to provide some cushion while still being firm enough to ensure stability.

- **Beam Work Fundamentals:**
  - *Mounts*: Starting a beam routine often involves a mount, which can vary from a simple step to a more complex acrobatic move. Proper technique in mounts sets the tone for the routine.
  - *Dismounts*: Ending a routine requires a controlled dismount. Common dismounts include flips, twists, and aerial maneuvers. Precision and control during the dismount are crucial for a successful performance.
- **Balancing Techniques:**
  - *Center of Gravity*: Maintaining the center of gravity over the beam is essential. Gymnasts need to adjust their body position continuously to stay balanced.
  - *Core Engagement*: A strong core is fundamental for beam routines. It helps stabilize the body and maintain alignment, reducing the risk of wobbling or falling.

FOOT PLACEMENT AND BODY CONTROL

Effective foot placement and body control are critical for maintaining balance and performing beam routines with precision.

- **Foot Placement:**
  - *Alignment*: Feet should be aligned parallel to the beam when walking or performing skills. Misalignment can lead to instability and potential falls.
  - *Contact Points*: The ball of the foot is typically the primary contact point with the beam. This allows for better control and stability.
- **Body Control:**
  - *Posture*: Maintaining an upright posture with shoulders back and head aligned is crucial. This helps in maintaining balance and executing skills with proper form.
  - *Arm Positioning*: Arms should be used for balance and counteracting movements. They should be held out to the sides or overhead as needed to aid in stability.
  - *Leg Movement*: Proper leg movement is essential for both balance and skill execution. Legs should be controlled and aligned to prevent unnecessary swaying or shifting.

BALANCING TECHNIQUE AND CREATIVITY

Balancing techniques on the beam involve a blend of precise movements and creative expression. Gymnasts must master technical skills while incorporating elements of artistry.

- **Balancing Techniques:**
  - *Static Balances*: Skills such as the arabesque or scale involve holding a stationary position on the beam.

These require excellent balance and core strength.
  - *Dynamic Movements*: Routines often include dynamic movements like leaps, turns, and jumps. Maintaining balance during these movements requires coordination and control.
  - *Transitions*: Smooth transitions between skills are vital. Gymnasts must seamlessly move from one element to another while maintaining balance.
- **Creativity in Routines:**
  - *Choreography*: Choreographing a beam routine involves integrating technical skills with creative elements. Music, rhythm, and artistic expression play a role in enhancing the performance.
  - *Personal Style*: Incorporating personal flair into routines can make performances stand out. This includes unique choreography, expressive movements, and innovative skills.

COMMON MISTAKES AND CORRECTIONS

Understanding common mistakes and their corrections is crucial for improving performance on the balance beam. Addressing these issues can help gymnasts enhance their routines and avoid penalties.

- **Common Mistakes:**
  - *Foot Wobbling*: Frequent wobbling or shifting of the feet can indicate poor balance. This often results from improper foot placement or lack of core engagement.
  - *Incorrect Body Alignment*: Poor alignment of the

body can lead to instability and falls. Misalignment typically occurs due to inadequate posture or body control.
  - *Over- or Under-Rotation*: Incomplete rotations or excessive rotation during skills can affect the routine's execution. This often results from improper technique or timing.
- **Corrections:**
  - *Improving Foot Placement*: Focus on precise foot placement and alignment. Practice balancing drills on the beam to enhance stability.
  - *Enhancing Body Control*: Strengthen the core and improve posture through targeted exercises. Regular practice of beam routines with attention to alignment can help in maintaining control.
  - *Refining Rotation Techniques*: Work on timing and technique for rotations. Use drills and practice routines to perfect the execution of skills and transitions.

TRAINING AND PRACTICE TIPS

To excel in balance beam routines, consistent training and practice are essential. Here are some tips for effective training:

- **Regular Practice:** Dedicate time to practice beam routines and specific skills. Consistent practice helps in building muscle memory and improving performance.
- **Use of Spotters:** When learning new skills, use spotters or safety equipment to prevent injuries. Spotters can

provide support and guidance during practice.

- **Visualization Techniques:** Visualizing routines and skills can enhance performance. Mental rehearsal helps in refining technique and building confidence.
- **Feedback and Coaching:** Work closely with a coach to receive feedback and make necessary adjustments. Coaches can provide valuable insights and corrections to improve performance.

The balance beam requires a combination of technical skill, strength, and artistry. By understanding the mechanics of beam work, focusing on foot placement and body control, and addressing common mistakes, gymnasts can enhance their performance and excel in this challenging apparatus. Regular practice, effective training strategies, and creative routines contribute to success on the balance beam, showcasing both athletic ability and artistic expression.

9

VAULT

THE VAULT IS ONE OF THE MOST EXCITING AND dynamic events in gymnastics, known for its explosive power and thrilling execution. It combines sprinting, explosive strength, and precise technique to launch off a springboard, perform aerial maneuvers, and land safely. This chapter explores the mechanics of the vault, methods for generating speed and power, landing techniques and safety considerations, and common mistakes with their corrections.

MECHANICS OF THE VAULT

Vaulting involves several stages, each crucial for a successful and impactful performance.

- **The Approach:**
    - *Run-Up*: The vault begins with a sprint down the runway. This phase is critical for building speed and momentum. Gymnasts must focus on maintaining

a consistent, powerful stride to maximize velocity.

- *Pre-Flight Phase*: As the gymnast reaches the springboard, they transition from running to jumping. Proper timing and coordination are essential to effectively transfer momentum from the run to the vault.

- **The Vault:**
  - *Springboard Contact*: Upon hitting the springboard, the gymnast uses its rebound to launch into the air. The springboard's purpose is to convert the gymnast's horizontal speed into vertical lift.
  - *Hand Contact with the Vault Table*: The next phase involves placing hands on the vault table. Gymnasts must strike the table with precision, using their hands to push off and rotate their body.
- **The Aerial Phase:**
  - *Flight*: After pushing off the vault table, the gymnast enters the flight phase. This is where the vault's complexity comes into play. Gymnasts perform twists, flips, or other aerial maneuvers while controlling their body position.
  - *Body Alignment*: Maintaining proper body alignment is crucial during the flight phase to ensure a clean and controlled landing. Gymnasts must focus on keeping their body tight and aligned.

GENERATING SPEED AND POWER

Speed and power are fundamental to a successful vault. Here's how gymnasts can enhance these elements:

- **Sprint Training:**
  - *Acceleration*: Building speed in the sprint phase requires effective acceleration techniques. Focus on explosive starts and increasing stride length and frequency.
  - *Strength Training*: Incorporate strength training exercises to enhance lower body power. Squats, lunges, and plyometric exercises can improve sprinting ability.
- **Vault Drills:**
  - *Run-Up Drills*: Practice sprints and run-up drills to build speed. Use resistance training tools like parachutes or sleds to improve explosive strength.
  - *Springboard Work*: Perform drills that focus on the transition from the sprint to the springboard. Emphasize timing and coordination to optimize the rebound effect.
- **Core and Upper Body Strength:**
  - *Upper Body Strength*: Strengthen the upper body to improve hand contact and push-off from the vault table. Exercises like push-ups and pull-ups are beneficial.
  - *Core Stability*: A strong core is essential for maintaining body alignment during the flight phase. Incorporate core exercises such as planks and Russian twists into your training routine.

LANDING TECHNIQUES AND SAFETY

A controlled landing is crucial for safety and scoring in vaulting. Here's how to achieve it:

- **Landing Techniques:**
  - *Controlled Descent*: As the gymnast approaches the mat, focus on a controlled descent. Prepare to absorb the impact by slightly bending the knees and keeping the body aligned.
  - *Stick the Landing*: Aim for a clean landing with minimal movement. Practice landing drills to improve precision and stability. A well-executed landing is vital for a high score and reduces the risk of injury.
- **Safety Considerations:**
  - *Use of Mats and Safety Equipment*: Always practice vaults with appropriate safety mats and equipment. Mats help cushion the impact and prevent injuries.
  - *Spotting and Supervision*: When learning new vaults, use spotters or coaches to provide guidance and ensure safe execution. Spotters can help correct form and provide support during practice.

COMMON MISTAKES AND CORRECTIONS

Understanding and correcting common mistakes can improve vault performance and prevent injuries.

- **Common Mistakes:**
  - *Insufficient Speed*: Not generating enough speed in the run-up can lead to a weak vault. This often results from poor sprinting technique or inadequate strength training.
  - *Poor Hand Placement*: Incorrect hand placement on the vault table can affect the push-off and flight

phase. This mistake typically arises from improper timing or technique.

- *Misaligned Body During Flight*: Body misalignment during the flight phase can result in a wobbly or off-center landing. This issue is often due to lack of control or incorrect aerial positioning.

- **Corrections:**
  - *Improving Speed*: Focus on enhancing sprinting technique and strength. Regularly practice acceleration drills and strength exercises to increase speed.
  - *Correct Hand Placement*: Work on drills that emphasize proper hand placement and push-off technique. Practice with guidance from a coach to ensure correct form.
  - *Enhancing Aerial Control*: Use visualizations and drills to improve body alignment during the flight phase. Practice aerial maneuvers in a controlled environment to build confidence and precision.

TRAINING AND PRACTICE TIPS

Effective training and practice are essential for mastering the vault. Consider these tips for improving performance:

- **Consistent Practice:** Regularly practice vaulting techniques and drills. Consistent practice helps in building muscle memory and improving execution.
- **Progressive Skill Development:** Gradually increase the complexity of skills and drills as proficiency improves. Begin with basic vaults and progress to more advanced

variations.

- **Feedback and Coaching:** Work closely with a coach to receive feedback and make necessary adjustments. Coaches can provide valuable insights and help refine technique.
- **Mental Preparation:** Visualization and mental rehearsal can enhance performance. Picture successful vaults and focus on executing skills with precision.

The vault is a dynamic and exciting event that requires a combination of speed, power, and technique. By understanding the mechanics of the vault, focusing on speed and power generation, mastering landing techniques, and addressing common mistakes, gymnasts can improve their performance and excel in this challenging apparatus. Regular practice, effective training strategies, and attention to safety contribute to success in vaulting, showcasing athletic ability and technical skill.

10

UNEVEN BARS

THE UNEVEN BARS IS A CAPTIVATING AND COMPLEX gymnastics apparatus that tests a gymnast's strength, technique, and creativity. It requires precision, control, and fluidity as gymnasts perform a series of swings, transitions, and release moves between two bars set at different heights. This chapter delves into the mechanics of bar swings, the importance of grip strength and core engagement, transition techniques and flight elements, and common mistakes with their corrections.

MECHANICS OF BAR SWINGS

Understanding the mechanics of bar swings is crucial for executing smooth and controlled routines on the uneven bars. The swing involves several key elements:

- **Swing Fundamentals:**
  - *Start Position*: Begin by grasping the bars with an overhand grip, arms fully extended, and body in a

hollow position. Ensure the shoulders are engaged and the core is tight.

- *Back Swing*: Initiate the swing by driving the legs backward while maintaining a strong core. The momentum generated from this action will propel the body forward.
- *Forward Swing*: As the legs swing forward, keep the body aligned and maintain a tight core. This phase requires a controlled release and an upward motion to prepare for the next move.

- **Timing and Rhythm:**
  - *Timing*: Proper timing is essential for achieving a smooth swing. Coordinate the timing of leg movements with the swing's momentum to maintain fluidity.
  - *Rhythm*: Establish a consistent rhythm to ensure the swing transitions smoothly between the back and forward phases. A steady rhythm aids in the execution of complex elements and transitions.
- **Release and Re-Grasp:**
  - *Release*: For release moves, execute a powerful push-off from the bars. This requires precise timing and coordination to achieve the desired height and trajectory.
  - *Re-Grasp*: After executing a release move, prepare for re-grasping the bars by positioning the hands accurately and timing the re-grasp with the body's descent.

GRIP STRENGTH AND CORE ENGAGEMENT

Grip strength and core engagement are fundamental to maintaining control and stability on the uneven bars.

- **Grip Strength:**
  - *Importance*: A strong grip is essential for holding onto the bars and executing various elements. Weak grip strength can result in instability and difficulty in performing moves.
  - *Exercises*: Incorporate grip-strengthening exercises such as dead hangs, wrist curls, and finger exercises into your training regimen. Use grip trainers or resistance bands to enhance grip strength.
- **Core Engagement:**
  - *Role*: Core engagement is crucial for maintaining body alignment and control during bar swings. A strong core stabilizes the body and improves overall performance.
  - *Core Exercises*: Include core-strengthening exercises like planks, leg raises, and hollow holds in your workout routine. Focus on exercises that target the abdominal muscles and lower back.

TRANSITION TECHNIQUES AND FLIGHT ELEMENTS

Transitions between different elements and flight maneuvers are critical components of a successful uneven bars routine.

- **Transition Techniques:**
  - *Kips and Casts*: Kips involve a powerful hip drive

to transition from a hanging position to a support position on the bar. Casts require a controlled swing to move from a low bar position to a high bar position.

  - *Handstands*: Achieving a handstand position is a key transition move. Focus on maintaining a straight body line and controlling the descent to facilitate smooth transitions.

- **Flight Elements:**
  - *Release Moves*: Release moves, such as the Tkatchev or Jaeger, involve releasing the bar and performing aerial maneuvers before re-grasping. Practice these moves with proper technique and timing to ensure a clean execution.
  - *Re-Grasp Techniques*: After a release move, prepare to re-grasp the bar by positioning the hands correctly and timing the re-grasp with the body's descent. Proper re-grasp technique ensures a smooth transition back to the bar.

COMMON MISTAKES AND CORRECTIONS

Identifying and correcting common mistakes can improve performance and reduce the risk of injury.

- **Common Mistakes:**
  - *Poor Grip Technique*: An improper grip or weak grip strength can lead to instability and difficulty in performing moves. Ensure a secure and correct grip on the bars.
  - *Inconsistent Timing*: Inconsistent timing during

swings and transitions can disrupt the flow of the routine. Practice maintaining a steady rhythm and coordinating movements.
    - *Incorrect Body Alignment*: Misalignment of the body during swings and transitions can affect control and execution. Focus on maintaining a straight body line and engaging the core.
- **Corrections:**
    - *Improve Grip Strength*: Incorporate grip-strengthening exercises and drills into your training routine. Use various grip techniques to enhance hand stability.
    - *Practice Timing*: Perform timing drills and use visualization techniques to improve rhythm and coordination. Work on synchronizing movements for a smoother routine.
    - *Focus on Alignment*: Use drills that emphasize body alignment and core engagement. Practice moves with proper form and receive feedback from a coach to refine technique.

TRAINING AND PRACTICE TIPS

Effective training and practice are essential for mastering the uneven bars. Consider these tips for improving performance:

- **Consistent Practice:** Regularly practice bar swings, transitions, and release moves. Consistent practice helps build muscle memory and improves execution.
- **Progressive Skill Development:** Gradually increase the complexity of skills and drills as proficiency improves.

Start with basic elements and progress to more advanced maneuvers.

- **Feedback and Coaching:** Work closely with a coach to receive feedback and make necessary adjustments. Coaches can provide valuable insights and help refine technique.
- **Safety and Spotting:** Use safety equipment and spotters when learning new skills. Spotters can provide guidance and ensure safe execution of complex maneuvers.

The uneven bars is a dynamic and challenging event that requires a combination of strength, technique, and creativity. By understanding the mechanics of bar swings, focusing on grip strength and core engagement, mastering transition techniques and flight elements, and addressing common mistakes, gymnasts can improve their performance and excel in this demanding apparatus. Regular practice, effective training strategies, and attention to safety contribute to success on the uneven bars, showcasing athletic ability and technical skill.

SECTION FOUR

ADVANCED TECHNIQUES AND TRAINING

11

ADVANCED TUMBLING AND AERIAL WORK

ADVANCED TUMBLING AND AERIAL WORK ARE essential aspects of gymnastics that challenge a gymnast's agility, strength, and coordination. This chapter focuses on mastering tumbling passes, developing aerial awareness and control, perfecting twisting techniques, and incorporating drills to enhance consistency. By honing these skills, gymnasts can elevate their performance and achieve a higher level of technical proficiency.

MASTERING TUMBLING PASSES

Tumbling passes are sequences of acrobatic movements performed in a continuous flow, showcasing a gymnast's power, precision, and creativity. Mastery of tumbling passes involves a combination of strength, technique, and rhythm.

- **Key Components:**
  - *Run-Up*: A powerful and controlled run-up generates

the necessary momentum for a successful tumbling pass. Focus on maintaining a strong and consistent pace while keeping the body aligned.

- *Takeoff*: The takeoff is crucial for launching into the tumbling sequence. Utilize explosive leg power and proper technique to achieve maximum height and control.
- *Execution*: During the tumbling pass, focus on maintaining proper body alignment, tight core engagement, and fluid transitions between movements. Common elements include handsprings, flips, and layouts.

- **Common Tumbling Passes:**
  - *Back Handspring*: A dynamic movement where the gymnast flips backward with a continuous motion. Practice the takeoff, back handspring, and landing to ensure smooth execution.

Back Handspring

  - *Layout*: A full-body extension in mid-air, where the gymnast maintains a straight body position. Emphasize proper body alignment and control during the layout phase.

Layout

- *Double Backflip*: A high-level tumbling pass involving two backflips in a single jump. This requires exceptional power, timing, and aerial awareness.

Double Backflip

AERIAL AWARENESS AND CONTROL

Aerial awareness and control are critical for executing complex moves and maintaining safety during advanced tumbling and aerial work.

- **Developing Aerial Awareness:**
  - *Spotting*: Learn to spot the ground or apparatus during aerial maneuvers. Spotting helps with orientation and improves the accuracy of landings.
  - *Body Positioning*: Understand and practice maintaining the correct body position during aerial work. This includes keeping the body aligned and using core engagement for stability.
  - *Visualization*: Use visualization techniques to mentally rehearse aerial maneuvers. Visualizing successful execution enhances confidence and improves performance.
- **Enhancing Control:**
  - *Controlled Landings*: Practice landing with control and precision. Focus on absorbing the impact through proper body alignment and knee flexion.
  - *Rotation Control*: Develop control over rotational movements by practicing drills that emphasize body rotation and positioning.

TWISTING TECHNIQUES

Twisting techniques add complexity and flair to tumbling passes and aerial work. Mastering twists involves precise control and coordination.

- **Basic Twisting Fundamentals:**
  - *Initiation*: Initiate the twist during the takeoff phase by using rotational momentum. Proper arm and leg positioning contributes to the twist's effectiveness.
  - *Mid-Air Control*: Maintain control over the twist by engaging the core and keeping the body tight. This prevents excessive rotation and ensures accurate execution.
  - *Landing*: Focus on landing with correct body alignment and balance after completing the twist. A controlled landing reduces the risk of injury and enhances performance.
- **Advanced Twisting Techniques:**
  - *Double Twists*: Perform two full twists during a single aerial maneuver. This requires advanced control and timing. Practice incrementally to build proficiency.
  - *Twisting Combinations*: Combine twists with other tumbling elements to create complex routines. Emphasize smooth transitions and precise execution of each component.

DRILLS TO IMPROVE CONSISTENCY

Consistency in advanced tumbling and aerial work is achieved through targeted drills and practice routines.

- **Tumbling Drills:**
  - *Drills for Power*: Use plyometric exercises such as box jumps and depth jumps to develop explosive power for tumbling passes.

- *Drills for Technique*: Practice individual tumbling elements, such as handsprings and layouts, to refine technique and improve execution.
- *Combination Drills*: Perform drills that combine multiple tumbling elements to build fluidity and consistency in routines.

- **Aerial Work Drills:**
  - *Aerial Awareness Drills*: Use drills such as trampoline work and aerial cartwheels to enhance spatial awareness and control.
  - *Twisting Drills*: Practice twisting drills on the trampoline or in a foam pit to build confidence and improve accuracy.
- **Safety Drills:**
  - *Spotting Practice*: Train with spotters or use safety equipment to practice new moves. Spotters help guide and ensure safe execution.
  - *Controlled Landings*: Use landing drills on soft surfaces to practice absorbing impact and landing with control.

TRAINING AND PRACTICE TIPS

Effective training and practice are essential for mastering advanced tumbling and aerial work. Consider these tips to enhance performance:

- **Regular Practice:** Consistently practice tumbling passes and aerial maneuvers to build muscle memory and improve performance.
- **Progressive Skill Development:** Gradually increase

the complexity of skills and routines as proficiency improves. Start with basic elements and progress to advanced techniques.

- **Feedback and Coaching:** Work closely with a coach to receive feedback and make necessary adjustments. Coaches provide valuable insights and help refine technique.
- **Safety and Spotting:** Use safety equipment and spotters when learning new skills. Spotters ensure safe execution and provide guidance during practice.

Advanced tumbling and aerial work are integral components of gymnastics that showcase a gymnast's agility, strength, and precision. By mastering tumbling passes, developing aerial awareness and control, perfecting twisting techniques, and incorporating targeted drills, gymnasts can enhance their performance and achieve a higher level of technical proficiency. Consistent practice, effective training strategies, and attention to safety contribute to success in advanced tumbling and aerial work, highlighting athletic ability and technical skill.

12

DEVELOPING STRENGTH AND FLEXIBILITY

STRENGTH AND FLEXIBILITY ARE FOUNDATIONAL elements for success in gymnastics. Both attributes contribute significantly to a gymnast's performance, technique, and overall safety. This chapter explores the role of strength training, flexibility routines, core stability, and strategies for injury prevention and rehabilitation.

THE ROLE OF STRENGTH TRAINING IN GYMNASTICS

Strength training is crucial for gymnasts to perform complex skills and routines effectively. It enhances overall performance, prevents injuries, and supports long-term athletic development.

- **Key Areas of Focus:**
  - *Upper Body Strength*: Essential for events like the uneven bars and rings, where pulling, lifting, and

holding body weight are fundamental. Exercises such as pull-ups, push-ups, and shoulder presses build upper body strength.

- *Lower Body Strength*: Important for vaulting, tumbling, and jumping. Squats, lunges, and plyometric exercises like box jumps help in developing explosive power and leg strength.
- *Grip Strength*: Crucial for maintaining hold on apparatuses like bars and rings. Gripping exercises, such as farmer's walks and dead hangs, enhance grip strength and endurance.
- *Functional Strength*: Exercises that mimic gymnastics movements, such as rope climbs and bodyweight drills, build functional strength and improve performance in specific routines.

- **Strength Training Techniques:**
  - *Progressive Overload*: Gradually increasing the resistance or intensity of exercises to build strength over time. This can be achieved by adding weight, increasing repetitions, or altering exercise variations.
  - *Bodyweight Exercises*: Utilizing body weight for resistance, including exercises like push-ups, pull-ups, and dips, is highly effective for gymnasts who need to control their own body weight.
  - *Resistance Training*: Incorporating resistance bands, free weights, and machines to target specific muscle groups and enhance overall strength.

FLEXIBILITY ROUTINES FOR ADVANCED GYMNASTS

Flexibility is vital for performing a wide range of gymnastics skills, from splits and jumps to intricate balance routines. Advanced gymnasts must maintain and improve their flexibility to achieve optimal performance and prevent injuries.

- **Key Flexibility Routines:**
  - *Dynamic Stretching*: Pre-training stretching that involves movement, such as leg swings and arm circles, to prepare muscles and joints for activity. This helps in increasing blood flow and range of motion.
  - *Static Stretching*: Post-training stretching where the position is held for a period, such as splits and hamstring stretches. This type of stretching helps in increasing flexibility and reducing muscle tension.
  - *PNF Stretching*: Proprioceptive Neuromuscular Facilitation involves contracting and relaxing muscles to enhance flexibility. This technique can improve range of motion and muscle length.
- **Flexibility Drills:**
  - *Splits*: Practice front and side splits regularly to improve hip and hamstring flexibility. Utilize supportive props and gradually increase the stretch over time.
  - *Backbends*: Exercises such as bridge poses and wheel poses help in developing spine flexibility and shoulder mobility, essential for routines requiring backbends and arches.

  - *Overhead Stretching*: Incorporate stretches that focus on shoulder and upper body flexibility, such as overhead tricep stretches and lat stretches, to improve range of motion for apparatus work.

CORE TRAINING AND STABILITY WORK

Core strength and stability are essential for maintaining proper body alignment, balance, and control during gymnastics routines. A strong core supports efficient movement and reduces the risk of injury.

- **Core Training Exercises:**
  - *Planks*: Front and side planks enhance core stability and strength. Aim to hold the plank position for extended periods and increase difficulty by adding variations.
  - *Leg Raises*: Effective for targeting the lower abdominal muscles. Perform lying leg raises or hanging leg raises to build core strength and endurance.
  - *Russian Twists*: A rotational exercise that engages the oblique muscles. Use a weight or medicine ball to increase resistance and improve rotational strength.
- **Stability Work:**
  - *Balance Drills*: Incorporate balance exercises such as single-leg stands and balance beam work to improve stability and control. Use tools like balance boards or stability balls for added challenge.
  - *Dynamic Core Exercises*: Exercises like mountain climbers and stability ball rollouts enhance core engagement while simulating dynamic movements.

INJURY PREVENTION AND REHABILITATION

Injury prevention and effective rehabilitation are crucial for maintaining long-term health and performance in gymnastics. Proper care and attention can help prevent common injuries and facilitate recovery when injuries occur.

- **Injury Prevention:**
  - *Warm-Up and Cool-Down*: Proper warm-up routines prepare the body for intense activity and reduce the risk of injury. Include dynamic stretching and mobility exercises before training and static stretching afterward.
  - *Technique and Form*: Emphasize correct technique and body mechanics during training to prevent overuse injuries and strains. Work with coaches to ensure proper form and alignment.
  - *Rest and Recovery*: Adequate rest and recovery time are essential for preventing overtraining and allowing the body to heal. Incorporate rest days and listen to the body's signals for fatigue or discomfort.
- **Rehabilitation Strategies:**
  - *Physical Therapy*: Engage in physical therapy to address specific injuries and improve recovery. Therapy may include targeted exercises, manual therapy, and modalities such as heat or ice.
  - *Gradual Return to Training*: Following an injury, return to training gradually to avoid re-injury. Focus on rebuilding strength and flexibility before resuming full-intensity workouts.

- *Cross-Training*: Incorporate low-impact activities, such as swimming or cycling, to maintain fitness while allowing injured areas to recover.

Strength and flexibility are fundamental aspects of gymnastics that contribute to performance, safety, and overall athleticism. By focusing on targeted strength training, implementing effective flexibility routines, enhancing core stability, and prioritizing injury prevention and rehabilitation, gymnasts can improve their skills and achieve greater success in their sport.

13

CONDITIONING FOR GYMNASTICS

CONDITIONING IS A CRITICAL ASPECT OF GYMNASTICS training, ensuring athletes possess the endurance, strength, and agility needed for their demanding routines. This chapter delves into cardiovascular conditioning, interval training, balancing strength with endurance, and strategies for monitoring progress and adjusting workouts to optimize performance and prevent overtraining.

CARDIOVASCULAR CONDITIONING FOR GYMNASTS

Cardiovascular conditioning is often less emphasized in gymnastics compared to sports like swimming or running, but it plays a crucial role in overall performance and stamina. A well-developed cardiovascular system supports efficient oxygen delivery to muscles, which is essential for maintaining high energy levels during routines and throughout training sessions.

- **Importance of Cardiovascular Fitness:**
    - *Enhanced Recovery*: Good cardiovascular fitness improves recovery times between high-intensity training sessions or competition events. Efficient blood flow helps in quicker removal of metabolic waste products and better nutrient delivery to muscles.
    - *Increased Stamina*: Gymnasts with strong cardiovascular systems can sustain high levels of activity and focus for longer periods, which is beneficial during extended training sessions and competitive performances.
- **Cardiovascular Conditioning Techniques:**
    - *Aerobic Exercises*: Incorporate steady-state activities like jogging, cycling, or rowing to build a solid aerobic base. Aim for 20-30 minutes of moderate-intensity aerobic exercise 2-3 times per week.
    - *High-Intensity Interval Training (HIIT):* Short bursts of intense activity followed by brief recovery periods can effectively improve cardiovascular fitness and simulate the demands of gymnastics routines. Examples include sprint intervals, circuit training, and plyometric drills.
    - *Sport-Specific Drills*: Include drills that mimic the movement patterns and intensity of gymnastics routines. For instance, integrating quick footwork drills or agility ladder exercises can enhance cardiovascular endurance relevant to gymnastics performance.

INTERVAL TRAINING FOR GYMNASTICS

Interval training is particularly effective for gymnasts because it combines high-intensity efforts with recovery periods, mimicking the stop-and-go nature of gymnastics routines. This training method improves both aerobic and anaerobic capacities, which are essential for sustaining energy and performing complex skills.

- **Benefits of Interval Training:**
  - *Improved Anaerobic Capacity*: Helps gymnasts develop the ability to perform at high intensities for short periods, crucial for explosive movements and routines.
  - *Enhanced Recovery*: Teaches the body to recover quickly between bouts of intense activity, which is beneficial during routines and training sessions.
- **Types of Interval Training:**
  - *High-Intensity Interval Training (HIIT):* Involves alternating between short bursts of maximum effort (e.g., 20-30 seconds) and periods of rest or low-intensity activity (e.g., 30-60 seconds). This can be applied to exercises like sprinting, jumping, or using cardio machines.
  - *Tabata Training*: A form of HIIT with 20 seconds of ultra-intense exercise followed by 10 seconds of rest, repeated for 4 minutes. This protocol can be adapted for gymnastics-specific movements or general conditioning.
  - *Circuit Training*: Incorporates multiple exercises performed in succession with minimal rest in

between. This can include a mix of strength, agility, and cardiovascular exercises tailored to gymnastics needs.

BALANCING STRENGTH AND ENDURANCE

In gymnastics, both strength and endurance are crucial for performance. Balancing these two components ensures gymnasts are not only powerful but also capable of sustaining their performance throughout their routines and competitions.

- **Strength vs. Endurance:**
  - *Strength*: Essential for executing powerful moves, maintaining control, and performing complex skills. Strength training should focus on exercises that build muscle and improve force production.
  - *Endurance*: Necessary for sustaining energy levels and maintaining technique over the duration of routines and training sessions. Endurance training should enhance the body's ability to perform consistently and recover quickly.
- **Training Balance:**
  - *Integrated Workouts*: Combine strength and endurance elements in a single workout session. For example, a circuit that includes bodyweight exercises (e.g., push-ups, squats) followed by cardio intervals (e.g., jumping jacks, high knees) can build both strength and endurance.
  - *Periodization*: Structure training cycles to emphasize different components at different times. For example,

focus on strength during the off-season and shift to endurance as competition approaches.

- *Cross-Training*: Engage in various forms of exercise to develop overall fitness. Activities such as swimming, running, or cycling can enhance cardiovascular endurance while complementing gymnastics-specific training.

MONITORING PROGRESS AND ADJUSTING WORKOUTS

Monitoring progress and adjusting workouts are essential for optimizing performance and preventing overtraining. Regular assessments help ensure that training remains effective and aligned with individual goals and needs.

- **Progress Monitoring:**
  - *Performance Metrics*: Track key performance indicators such as strength levels, endurance capacity, and skill execution. Use tools like performance logs or fitness trackers to record and analyze data.
  - *Feedback*: Regularly assess technique and progress with the help of coaches or trainers. Video analysis can provide valuable insights into form and execution.
- **Adjusting Workouts:**
  - *Progressive Overload*: Gradually increase the intensity, duration, or difficulty of workouts to continue making gains. This might involve adding weight, increasing intervals, or introducing new exercises.

- *Recovery and Rest*: Adjust workout intensity based on recovery needs and signs of fatigue. Incorporate rest days and lighter training sessions to allow for proper recovery and prevent burnout.
- *Individualization*: Tailor workouts to the individual's specific needs, strengths, and areas for improvement. Personalize training plans to address particular goals or challenges.

Conditioning in gymnastics involves a holistic approach that integrates cardiovascular and interval training, balances strength with endurance, and emphasizes progress monitoring and adjustment. By focusing on these aspects, gymnasts can enhance their performance, maintain peak physical condition, and achieve their athletic goals.

SECTION FIVE

NUTRITION, RECOVERY, AND MENTAL PREPARATION

14

NUTRITION FOR GYMNASTS

NUTRITION IS A CORNERSTONE OF SUCCESSFUL gymnastics training and performance. A well-balanced diet not only fuels workouts but also supports recovery, injury prevention, and overall health. This chapter delves into the specifics of nutrition tailored to gymnasts, including meal planning, hydration strategies, and the effective use of supplements.

ENERGY REQUIREMENTS

- **Caloric Needs:** Gymnasts typically require a higher caloric intake due to the demanding nature of their training. The exact number varies depending on age, body size, gender, training intensity, and goals. Generally, gymnasts need between 2,000 and 4,000 calories per day.
- **Macronutrient Balance:**
    - *Carbohydrates*: Provide the primary source of energy. They should constitute 45-65% of the daily calorie intake. Examples include whole grains, fruits, vegetables, and legumes.

- *Proteins*: Crucial for muscle repair and growth, proteins should make up about 10-35% of daily calories. Sources include lean meats, dairy products, eggs, and plant-based options like tofu and beans.
- *Fats*: Essential for overall health, fats should account for 20-35% of daily calories. Focus on healthy fats from avocados, nuts, seeds, and olive oil.

NUTRIENT TIMING

- **Pre-Training:** A meal or snack rich in carbohydrates and moderate in protein should be consumed 1-2 hours before training. Options include oatmeal with berries, a whole-grain sandwich with lean protein, or a smoothie with banana and yogurt.
- **Post-Training:** To aid recovery, consume a combination of carbohydrates and protein within 30 minutes to 2 hours post-exercise. Examples include a protein shake with fruit, a chicken wrap with vegetables, or Greek yogurt with honey.

MICRONUTRIENTS

- **Vitamins:** Essential for energy production and immune function. Key vitamins include vitamin D (for bone health), vitamin C (for immune support), and B vitamins (for energy metabolism).
- **Minerals:** Important for muscle function and bone health. Focus on calcium (from dairy products or fortified plant milks), iron (from lean meats and spinach), and magnesium (from nuts and seeds).

BUILDING A NUTRITIONAL PLAN FOR TRAINING AND COMPETITION

1. Daily Meal Planning:

- **Breakfast:** Start the day with a balanced meal that includes complex carbohydrates, protein, and healthy fats. Examples: Whole-grain cereal with milk and fruit, or eggs with avocado on whole-grain toast.
- **Lunch:** Combine lean proteins, whole grains, and vegetables. Examples: Grilled chicken salad with quinoa, or a turkey and vegetable wrap.
- **Dinner:** Focus on a balanced plate with protein, carbs, and vegetables. Examples: Baked salmon with sweet potato and steamed broccoli, or stir-fried tofu with brown rice and mixed vegetables.
- **Snacks:** Include healthy snacks to maintain energy levels between meals. Examples: A handful of almonds, apple slices with peanut butter, or a small bowl of cottage cheese with fruit.

2. Competition Nutrition:

- **Pre-Competition:** Choose easily digestible foods that provide quick energy. Avoid heavy, fatty, or high-fiber foods that might cause discomfort. Examples: A banana, a granola bar, or a small serving of rice pudding.
- **During Competition:** For longer events, carry portable snacks that provide energy without being overly filling. Options include energy bars, dried fruit, or electrolyte-rich drinks.
- **Post-Competition:** Focus on recovery by consuming

a meal or snack that replenishes glycogen stores and supports muscle repair. Examples: A smoothie with protein powder and fruit, or a chicken and vegetable stir-fry with brown rice.

3. Personalized Needs:

- **Preferences and Lifestyle:** Tailor the nutritional plan to individual preferences and lifestyle. Ensure the diet is enjoyable and sustainable, which enhances adherence.
- **Allergies and Intolerances:** Adapt the plan to accommodate any food allergies or intolerances, ensuring that all nutritional needs are still met.

HYDRATION STRATEGIES FOR GYMNASTS

1. Daily Fluid Intake:

- **General Guidelines:** Aim for 8-10 cups (2-2.5 liters) of water per day. The actual requirement may increase based on training intensity and environmental conditions.
- **Pre-Training Hydration:** Drink about 500 ml (17 oz) of water 2 hours before training to ensure adequate hydration.
- **During Training:** Sip water regularly throughout the session, especially if it lasts more than an hour. For prolonged sessions, consider drinks with electrolytes.

2. Monitoring Hydration:

- **Urine Color:** Use urine color as a hydration indicator. Pale yellow typically suggests adequate hydration, while dark yellow indicates the need for more fluids.

- **Thirst:** Drink when thirsty, but also proactively hydrate, especially during and after intense training sessions.

Proper dietary practices support not only physical performance but also long-term well-being, allowing gymnasts to achieve their full potential in the sport.

15

RECOVERY AND INJURY PREVENTION

RECOVERY AND INJURY PREVENTION ARE CRITICAL components of a gymnast's training regimen. Effective recovery strategies help athletes repair muscle tissue, restore energy levels, and prevent injuries, ensuring longevity and peak performance in the sport. This chapter covers the essential aspects of recovery, strategies to manage soreness and fatigue, common injuries in gymnastics, and effective recovery techniques.

THE IMPORTANCE OF REST AND RECOVERY

1. Recovery Basics:

- **Muscle Repair:** Intense training causes micro-tears in muscle fibers. Recovery allows these fibers to repair and strengthen, improving overall performance and reducing the risk of overuse injuries.
- **Energy Restoration:** Recovery replenishes depleted energy stores, particularly glycogen, which is essential

for sustained performance and prevents fatigue.

- **Mental Refreshment:** Adequate rest helps reduce mental fatigue, improving focus, motivation, and reducing the risk of burnout.

2. Recovery Time:

- **Daily Recovery:** Incorporates periods of low-intensity activity or rest between intense training sessions. Aim for at least one full rest day per week.
- **Post-Training Recovery:** Implement cool-down exercises and stretching immediately after training to aid in the recovery process.
- **Sleep:** Ensure 7-9 hours of quality sleep per night. Sleep is crucial for physical and mental recovery, hormone regulation, and overall health.

MANAGING MUSCLE SORENESS AND FATIGUE

1. Types of Muscle Soreness:

- **Acute Soreness:** Felt immediately after exercise and typically subsides within a few hours. This is usually due to lactic acid buildup.
- **Delayed Onset Muscle Soreness (DOMS):** Occurs 24-48 hours after intense exercise, resulting from micro-tears in muscles. This is common after introducing new exercises or increasing intensity.

2. Strategies for Managing Soreness:

- **Active Recovery:** Engage in low-intensity activities that help increase blood flow to sore muscles, promoting faster recovery.

- **Stretching and Mobility:** Gentle stretching and mobility exercises can alleviate tightness and improve flexibility.
- **Hydration:** Maintain proper hydration to support muscle function and recovery. Drink water regularly throughout the day, especially before and after training.

3. Addressing Fatigue:

- **Balanced Nutrition:** Consuming a well-balanced diet with adequate carbohydrates, proteins, and fats helps restore energy levels and supports muscle repair.
- **Sleep Quality:** Prioritize good sleep hygiene, including a consistent sleep schedule and a restful environment, to combat fatigue and improve recovery.

COMMON GYMNASTICS INJURIES AND HOW TO PREVENT THEM

1. Common Injuries:

- **Sprains and Strains:** Often occur due to overstretching or excessive force. Common in the ankles, wrists, and shoulders.
- **Stress Fractures:** Result from repetitive stress or impact, commonly affecting the lower back and feet.
- **Tendinitis:** Inflammation of tendons due to overuse, typically seen in the shoulders, elbows, and knees.
- **Dislocations:** Occur when a joint is forced out of its normal position, frequently affecting the shoulders and fingers.

2. Prevention Strategies:

- **Proper Technique:** Emphasize correct technique and form to reduce the risk of injury. Work with coaches to ensure exercises are performed correctly.
- **Strength and Flexibility:** Regularly engage in strength training and flexibility exercises to support joints and muscles, reducing the risk of injuries.
- **Gradual Progression:** Increase training intensity and complexity gradually to allow the body to adapt and reduce the risk of overuse injuries.

THE ROLE OF RECOVERY TECHNIQUES

1. Massage Therapy:

- **Benefits:** Helps to reduce muscle tension, improve blood circulation, and promote relaxation. Can also aid in the breakdown of scar tissue and improve flexibility.
- **Types of Massage:** Includes techniques like Swedish massage for overall relaxation and deep tissue massage for targeted muscle relief.

2. Ice Baths and Cryotherapy:

- **Ice Baths:** Involve immersing the body in cold water to reduce inflammation and muscle soreness. Recommended for 10-15 minutes after intense training sessions.
- **Cryotherapy:** Utilizes extreme cold to reduce inflammation and promote muscle recovery. Can be applied locally or through whole-body cryotherapy chambers.

4. Other Recovery Techniques:

- **Foam Rolling:** A form of self-myofascial release that helps to release muscle tightness and improve blood flow. Recommended for daily use or as part of a warm-up/cool-down routine.
- **Hydrotherapy:** Utilizes water-based exercises and treatments to support recovery. Includes techniques like water jogging or resistance exercises in a pool.

A well-rounded approach to recovery not only supports physical repair but also contributes to mental well-being and overall athletic success.

16

MENTAL CONDITIONING AND FOCUS

IN GYMNASTICS, MENTAL CONDITIONING IS AS CRUCIAL as physical training. The ability to maintain focus, handle pressure, and remain motivated can significantly impact performance and overall success. This chapter delves into strategies for building mental toughness, employing visualization techniques, managing competition anxiety, and staying motivated during rigorous training.

BUILDING MENTAL TOUGHNESS FOR GYMNASTICS

1. Understanding Mental Toughness:

- **Definition:** Mental toughness refers to the ability to remain resilient, focused, and confident in the face of challenges and pressure. It is essential for overcoming obstacles, handling stress, and performing under competitive conditions.
- **Components:** Key elements include self-confidence,

emotional control, and the ability to stay focused despite distractions or setbacks.

2. Developing Mental Toughness:

- **Goal Setting:** Establish clear, achievable goals to provide direction and motivation. Break these goals into smaller, manageable steps to track progress and build confidence.
- **Resilience Training:** Practice dealing with setbacks and failures by analyzing what went wrong and developing strategies for improvement. Embrace challenges as opportunities for growth.
- **Positive Self-Talk:** Replace negative thoughts with positive affirmations. Encourage yourself with statements that reinforce your abilities and strengths.
- **Stress Management Techniques:** Engage in relaxation exercises, such as deep breathing or progressive muscle relaxation, to manage stress and maintain focus during training and competition.

3. Routine and Discipline:

- **Consistency:** Develop a consistent training routine to build discipline and familiarity. Adhering to a structured schedule helps in establishing habits and mental resilience.
- **Practice Under Pressure:** Simulate competition conditions during practice sessions to get accustomed to performing under pressure. This helps in adapting to the stress and demands of actual competitions.

DEALING WITH COMPETITION ANXIETY

1. Understanding Competition Anxiety:

- **Definition:** Competition anxiety is the nervousness or fear experienced before and during competitive events. It can affect performance if not managed effectively.
- **Symptoms:** Common signs include increased heart rate, sweating, negative thoughts, and physical tension.

2. Strategies to Manage Anxiety:

- **Pre-Competition Preparation:** Develop a pre-competition routine that includes relaxation techniques, warm-ups, and mental preparation to reduce anxiety and enhance focus.
- **Breathing Exercises:** Practice deep breathing exercises to calm the nervous system and reduce physical symptoms of anxiety. Focus on slow, deep breaths to relax and center yourself.
- **Focus on the Process:** Concentrate on the elements of your performance rather than the outcome. By focusing on executing each movement, you can shift attention away from anxiety and towards your performance.
- **Confidence Building:** Reinforce your self-confidence by recalling past successes and positive training experiences. Remind yourself of your preparation and abilities.

3. Seeking Support:

- **Coaching Support:** Communicate with your coach about your anxiety and seek their guidance and encouragement. Coaches can provide valuable support

and help you develop strategies to manage stress.

- **Mental Health Professionals:** If anxiety becomes overwhelming, consider working with a sports psychologist or mental health professional who specializes in performance anxiety.

Mental conditioning plays a crucial role in gymnastics, impacting performance, confidence, and overall success. By building mental toughness, managing competition anxiety, and staying motivated, gymnasts can enhance their performance and resilience. Incorporating these mental conditioning strategies into training routines can lead to improved focus, reduced stress, and greater overall achievement in the sport.

SECTION SIX

COMPETITIVE GYMNASTICS

17

PREPARING FOR COMPETITIONS

GYMNASTICS COMPETITIONS ARE THE CULMINATION of countless hours of practice and dedication. Preparing for a meet involves not just physical readiness but also mental and logistical preparation. This chapter will guide you through the essential steps to ensure you are fully prepared for your first competition and beyond.

THE PATH TO YOUR FIRST COMPETITION

1. Training and Preparation:

- **Consistent Training:** Follow a structured training plan leading up to the competition. Focus on perfecting your routines and addressing any areas of weakness.
- **Mock Competitions:** Participate in mock meets or practice competitions to simulate the conditions of the actual event. This will help you acclimate to performing under pressure and manage competition anxiety.

2. Practical Preparations:

- **Register for the Meet:** Ensure you complete all necessary registration paperwork and meet entry deadlines. Confirm your participation and receive any relevant information about the competition.
- **Prepare Your Gear:** Check that all your equipment, leotards, and accessories are in good condition and packed well ahead of time. This includes grips, chalk, and any personal items you'll need.

WHAT TO EXPECT AT A GYMNASTICS MEET

1. Arrival and Check-In:

- **Arrival Time:** Arrive at the venue well in advance to allow time for check-in, warming up, and familiarizing yourself with the competition environment.
- **Check-In Process:** Check in with the meet officials to receive your competition number, schedule, and any additional instructions. This is also a good time to address any last-minute concerns.

2. Venue Layout:

- **Orientation:** Take a moment to explore the venue, noting the location of the competition floor, warm-up areas, restrooms, and any other relevant facilities.
- **Warm-Up Areas:** Identify where you can warm up and practice before your routines. This space is crucial for preparing physically and mentally before competing.

3. Competition Flow:

- **Event Schedule:** Familiarize yourself with the schedule for your events, including warm-up times and performance slots. Be mindful of any changes or announcements made by the meet officials.
- **Routine Performance:** Each gymnast will perform their routines in a specific order. Be prepared for any delays or adjustments in the schedule and stay focused on your performance.

The support of coaches and teammates also plays a vital role in navigating the competition environment and achieving success.

18

NURTURING THE NEXT OLYMPIC GYMNAST

RAISING A FUTURE OLYMPIC GYMNAST REQUIRES dedication, structure, and support. Gymnastics is an intense sport that demands both physical and mental strength, and parents play a crucial role in helping young athletes navigate this challenging journey. While the road to the Olympics is long, it is filled with opportunities for growth, resilience, and success. Here's how to best support and guide your child's path to becoming a top-level gymnast.

Early Engagement: Laying the Foundation

Introducing gymnastics at a young age, typically between 3-4 years old, is critical to building foundational skills like balance, coordination, and flexibility. Early exposure should emphasize fun and enjoyment, not competition. Engaging in fun activities like basic rolls, jumps, and balancing games will encourage your child's interest in gymnastics without overwhelming them.

It's important to select a gym that has experienced,

certified coaches with a track record of developing gymnasts. The right facility should prioritize safety, skill development, and fun, helping children cultivate both their technical abilities and a love for the sport.

Nurturing Passion and Avoiding Pressure

While gymnastics should be a focus, allow your child to explore other sports and activities. Cross-training in sports like swimming or soccer can complement their gymnastics training while keeping things fresh and exciting. This broad athletic experience helps prevent burnout and fosters a well-rounded athlete.

Recognize and celebrate the small achievements along the way. Instead of focusing on competition results, celebrate progress in skills and personal growth. This fosters resilience and helps your child develop a healthy relationship with the sport.

STRUCTURED TRAINING AND PROFESSIONAL GUIDANCE

As your child progresses, their training will need to become more structured. Young gymnasts (ages 5-7) may train two to three times a week, with intensity increasing as they grow older. By the time they are teenagers, serious competitors may train 30-40 hours a week. It's important to ensure that their training plan is balanced to avoid overtraining and injury.

Olympic-level gymnastics demands expert coaching. Seek coaches with competitive experience who understand the mental and physical demands of the sport. They should

provide structured training that includes technical skill development, conditioning, and mental preparation.

NUTRITION AND RECOVERY

Proper nutrition is essential for supporting intense gymnastics training. A balanced diet that includes lean proteins, complex carbohydrates, healthy fats, fruits, and vegetables is key. Gymnasts should be educated on making healthy food choices that fuel their bodies for both training and recovery. Hydration is equally important—ensure your child drinks enough water before, during, and after training.

Rest is critical to a gymnast's success. Make sure your child gets enough sleep and recovery time, especially after intense training or competitions. Rest days allow muscles to repair and help prevent overuse injuries. Recovery techniques like stretching, massage, and ice baths can also help manage muscle soreness and fatigue.

INJURY PREVENTION AND PROPER TECHNIQUE

Injury prevention starts with teaching proper techniques early. Good coaches emphasize the importance of safe landings, proper form, and controlled movements. Overuse injuries are common in gymnastics, so maintaining a well-structured training plan that includes rest is vital.

If an injury occurs, it's essential to address it immediately. Pushing through injuries can worsen the problem. Consult with a sports medicine specialist and follow a structured rehabilitation plan before returning to full training.

BALANCING GYMNASTICS WITH LIFE

As gymnastics becomes more competitive, it's essential to balance training with schoolwork and social activities. Time management is key to preventing your child from feeling overwhelmed. Encourage hobbies and friendships outside the sport to promote a well-rounded, happy life.

The road to the Olympics is a marathon, not a sprint. Celebrate your child's effort, growth, and passion for gymnastics, regardless of competition results. Creating a positive, supportive environment will help your child remain motivated and excited about the sport.

Raising a future Olympic gymnast requires a blend of early engagement, structured training, mental conditioning, and a strong support system. It's essential to foster passion and resilience while ensuring that the journey remains enjoyable and balanced. By providing the right support, parents can help their child reach their full potential—whether that's on the Olympic stage or simply enjoying a lifelong love of gymnastics.

19

FILIPINO OLYMPIANS IN GYMNASTICS: BALANCING DREAMS AND REALITY

GYMNASTICS, A SPORT THAT COMBINES GRACE, strength, and precision, has gained attention in the Philippines over the years, thanks to the incredible dedication of Filipino gymnasts who have represented the country on the Olympic stage. Though gymnastics may not be as celebrated as some other sports in the Philippines, its athletes have demonstrated exceptional resilience and potential, inspiring future generations to pursue excellence in this physically demanding discipline.

EARLY BEGINNINGS

The Philippines has a long yet often overlooked history in gymnastics, with athletes participating in various international competitions over the decades. However, it wasn't until recent years that Filipino gymnasts began to emerge as competitive contenders on the world stage, including the Olympics. Despite limited funding and resources, the passion for gymnastics has quietly grown in the Philippines, with athletes continuously working to refine their skills and bring honor to the country.

The first Filipino gymnast to qualify for the Olympic Games was **Bea Lucero**, who competed in the 1984 Los Angeles Olympics. Lucero's participation marked a significant milestone for Filipino gymnastics, as she opened doors for future gymnasts to dream of competing in the world's biggest sporting event. While Lucero did not win a medal, her presence in the Olympics was a testament to the perseverance of Filipino athletes, inspiring future gymnasts to push the limits of their potential.

CARLOS YULO

No discussion of Filipino gymnastics would be complete without highlighting the exceptional achievements of **Carlos Edriel Yulo**, the country's most decorated and successful gymnast to date. Born in Manila, Yulo has become a household name in Philippine sports, thanks to his meteoric rise in the world of gymnastics. His journey to Olympic glory began at a young age when he started training at the Gymnastics Association of the Philippines (GAP), eventually earning a scholarship to train in Japan under the guidance of celebrated coach Munehiro Kugimiya.

Carlos Yulo

In 2019, Yulo made history by becoming the first Filipino gymnast to win a gold medal at the **World Artistic Gymnastics Championships** in Stuttgart, Germany. Competing in the men's floor exercise, Yulo stunned the world with his precision, power, and flawless execution, earning him a score that placed him at the top of the podium. His victory was a landmark achievement not only for Filipino gymnastics but also for Southeast Asian athletes, as Yulo became the first from the region to win a world title in the sport.

Yulo's success on the world stage secured him a spot at the **2020 Tokyo Olympics**, where the Filipino gymnast hoped to continue his winning streak. In the men's all-around event, Yulo put up a commendable performance, though he narrowly missed the podium in the floor exercise

Carlos Yulo at the 2019 SEA Games

event, finishing fourth. Despite the setback, Yulo's Olympic journey was far from over, and he vowed to come back stronger in future competitions. His drive and determination have made him a symbol of hope for the sport of gymnastics in the Philippines.

In response to Yulo's historic victories, the Philippine government, through the **Philippine Sports Commission (PSC)** and various private sponsors, has begun to offer more substantial support for gymnastics. This increased focus on gymnastics development is a promising step toward ensuring that future generations of Filipino athletes can compete at the highest levels without the barriers faced by their predecessors.

WOMEN'S GYMNASTICS: PROMISING TALENTS ON THE RISE

While men's gymnastics, led by Carlos Yulo, has taken center stage in the Philippines, the country also has several talented female gymnasts working hard to make their mark on the international scene. **Kaitlin de Guzman**, a Filipino-American gymnast, is one such athlete who has shown potential in recent years. De Guzman won a gold medal in the uneven bars at the 2017 Southeast Asian (SEA) Games, signaling her potential to compete at higher levels of the sport.

Philippine Sports Commission logo

In recent years, the Gymnastics Association of the Philippines has ramped up efforts to identify and nurture young talent across the country. With Carlos Yulo as a role model, the next generation of Filipino gymnasts is more determined than ever to reach the top. Aspiring gymnasts are now training with the hopes of one day representing the Philippines at the Olympics, and with better infrastructure and coaching, the country's prospects in gymnastics continue to grow.

THE FUTURE OF FILIPINO GYMNASTICS

The future of Filipino gymnastics is bright, thanks to the trailblazing efforts of Carlos Yulo and the growing interest in the sport. Yulo's journey from humble beginnings in Manila to winning world championships and competing at the Olympics has shown that Filipino athletes can excel in gymnastics on the global stage.

LIST OF OLYMPIC MEDALISTS (2000-2024)

MEN

All-around, individual

Games	Gold	Silver	Bronze
2000 Sydney	Alexei Nemov Russia	Yang Wei China	Oleksandr Beresh Ukraine
2004 Athens	Paul Hamm United States	Kim Dae-eun South Korea	Yang Tae-young South Korea
2008 Beijing	Yang Wei China	Kōhei Uchimura Japan	Benoît Caranobe France
2012 London	Kōhei Uchimura Japan	Marcel Nguyen Germany	Danell Leyva United States
2016 Rio de Janeiro	Kōhei Uchimura Japan	Oleg Verniaiev Ukraine	Max Whitlock Great Britain
2020 Tokyo	Daiki Hashimoto Japan	Xiao Ruoteng China	Nikita Nagornyy ROC
2024 Paris	Shinnosuke Oka Japan	Zhang Boheng China	Xiao Ruoteng China

All-around, Teams

Games	Gold	Silver	Bronze
2000 Sydney	China (CHN) Huang Xu Li Xiaopeng Xiao Junfeng Xing Aowei Yang Wei Zheng Lihui	Ukraine(UKR) Alexander Beresch Valeriy Honcharov Ruslan Mezentsev Valeri Pereshkura Olexander Svitlichni Roman Zozulya	Russia (RUS) Maxim Aleshin Alexei Bondarenko Dmitri Drevin Nikolai Kryukov Alexei Nemov Yevgeni Podgorny
2004 Athens	Japan (JPN) Takehiro Kashima Hisashi Mizutori Daisuke Nakano Hiroyuki Tomita Naoya Tsukahara Isao Yoneda	United States (USA) Jason Gatson Morgan Hamm Paul Hamm Brett McClure Blaine Wilson Guard Young	Romania(ROU) Marian Drăgulescu Ilie Daniel Popescu Dan Nicolae Potra Răzvan Dorin Şelariu Ioan Silviu Suciu Marius Urzică
2008 Beijing	China (CHN) Chen Yibing Huang Xu Li Xiaopeng Xiao Qin Yang Wei Zou Kai	Japan(JPN) Takehiro Kashima Takuya Nakase Makoto Okiguchi Koki Sakamoto Hiroyuki Tomita Kōhei Uchimura	United States (USA) Alexander Artemev Raj Bhavsar Joe Hagerty Jonathan Horton Justin Spring Kai Wen Tan

Games	Gold	Silver	Bronze
2012 London	China (CHN) Chen Yibing Feng Zhe Guo Weiyang Zhang Chenglong Zou Kai	Japan(JPN) Ryohei Kato Kazuhito Tanaka Yusuke Tanaka Kōhei Uchimura Koji Yamamuro	Great Britain (GBR) Sam Oldham Daniel Purvis Louis Smith Kristian Thomas Max Whitlock
2016 Rio de Janeiro	Japan (JPN) Kenzō Shirai Yūsuke Tanaka Koji Yamamuro Kōhei Uchimura Ryōhei Katō	Russia(RUS) Denis Ablyazin David Belyavskiy Ivan Stretovich Nikolai Kuksenkov Nikita Nagornyy	China(CHN) Deng Shudi Lin Chaopan Liu Yang You Hao Zhang Chenglong
2020 Tokyo	ROC (ROC) Denis Ablyazin David Belyavskiy Artur Dalaloyan Nikita Nagornyy	Japan(JPN) Daiki Hashimoto Kazuma Kaya Takeru Kitazono Wataru Tanigawa	China(CHN) Lin Chaopan Sun Wei Xiao Ruoteng Zou Jingyuan
2024 Paris	Japan (JPN) Daiki Hashimoto Kazuma Kaya Shinnosuke Oka Takaaki Sugino Wataru Tanigawa	China(CHN) Liu Yang Su Weide Xiao Ruoteng Zhang Boheng Zou Jingyuan	United States (USA) Asher Hong Paul Juda Brody Malone Stephen Nedoroscik Fred Richard

Floor Exercise

Games	Gold	Silver	Bronze
2000 Sydney	Igors Vihrovs Latvia	Alexei Nemov Russia	Yordan Yovchev Bulgaria
2004 Athens	Kyle Shewfelt Canada	Marian Drăgulescu Romania	Yordan Yovchev Bulgaria
2008 Beijing	Zou Kai China	Gervasio Deferr Spain	Anton Golotsutskov Russia
2012 London	Zou Kai China	Kōhei Uchimura Japan	Denis Ablyazin Russia
2016 Rio de Janeiro	Max Whitlock Great Britain	Diego Hypólito Brazil	Arthur Mariano Brazil
2020 Tokyo	Artem Dolgopyat Israel	Rayderley Zapata Spain	Xiao Ruoteng China
2024 Paris	Carlos Yulo Philippines	Artem Dolgopyat Israel	Jake Jarman Great Britain

Horizontal Bar

Games	Gold	Silver	Bronze
2000 Sydney	Alexei Nemov Russia	Benjamin Varonian France	Lee Joo-Hyung South Korea
2004 Athens	Igor Cassina Italy	Paul Hamm United States	Isao Yoneda Japan
2008 Beijing	Zou Kai China	Jonathan Horton United States	Fabian Hambüchen Germany

Games	Gold	Silver	Bronze
2012 London	Epke Zonderland Netherlands	Fabian Hambüchen Germany	Zou Kai China
2016 Rio de Janeiro	Fabian Hambüchen Germany	Danell Leyva United States	Nile Wilson Great Britain
2020 Tokyo	Daiki Hashimoto Japan	Tin Srbić Croatia	Nikita Nagornyy ROC
2024 Paris	Shinnosuke Oka Japan	Ángel Barajas Colombia	Tang Chia-hung Chinese Taipei Zhang Boheng China

Parallel Bars

Games	Gold	Silver	Bronze
2000 Sydney	Li Xiaopeng China	Lee Joo-Hyung South Korea	Alexei Nemov Russia
2004 Athens	Valeriy Honcharov Ukraine	Hiroyuki Tomita Japan	Li Xiaopeng China
2008 Beijing	Li Xiaopeng China	Yoo Won-Chul South Korea	Anton Fokin Uzbekistan
2012 London	Feng Zhe China	Marcel Nguyen Germany	Hamilton Sabot France
2016 Rio de Janeiro	Oleg Verniaiev Ukraine	Danell Leyva United States	David Belyavskiy Russia
2020 Tokyo	Zou Jingyuan China	Lukas Dauser Germany	Ferhat Arican Turkey
2024 Paris	Zou Jingyuan China	Illia Kovtun Ukraine	Shinnosuke Oka Japan

Pommel Horse

Games	Gold	Silver	Bronze
2000 Sydney	Marius Urzică Romania	Eric Poujade France	Alexei Nemov Russia
2004 Athens	Teng Haibin China	Marius Urzică Romania	Takehiro Kashima Japan
2008 Beijing	Xiao Qin China	Filip Ude Croatia	Louis Smith Great Britain
2012 London	Krisztián Berki Hungary	Louis Smith Great Britain	Max Whitlock Great Britain
2016 Rio de Janeiro	Max Whitlock Great Britain	Louis Smith Great Britain	Alexander Naddour United States
2020 Tokyo	Max Whitlock Great Britain	Lee Chih-kai Chinese Taipei	Kazuma Kaya Japan
2024 Paris	Rhys McClenaghan Ireland	Nariman Kurbanov Kazakhstan	Stephen Nedoroscik United States

Rings

Games	Gold	Silver	Bronze
2000 Sydney	Szilveszter Csollány Hungary	Dimosthenis Tampakos Greece	Yordan Yovchev Bulgaria
2004 Athens	Dimosthenis Tampakos Greece	Yordan Yovchev Bulgaria	Jury Chechi Italy
2008 Beijing	Chen Yibing China	Yang Wei China	Oleksandr Vorobiov Ukraine

Games	Gold	Silver	Bronze
2012 London	Arthur Zanetti Brazil	Chen Yibing China	Matteo Morandi Italy
2016 Rio de Janeiro	Eleftherios Petrounias Greece	Arthur Zanetti Brazil	Denis Ablyazin Russia
2020 Tokyo	Liu Yang China	You Hao China	Eleftherios Petrounias Greece
2024 Paris	Liu Yang China	Zou Jingyuan China	Eleftherios Petrounias Greece

Vault

Games	Gold	Silver	Bronze
2000 Sydney	Gervasio Deferr Spain	Alexei Bondarenko Russia	Leszek Blanik Poland
2004 Athens	Gervasio Deferr Spain	Jevgēņijs Sapronenko Latvia	Marian Drăgulescu Romania
2008 Beijing	Leszek Blanik Poland	Thomas Bouhail France	Anton Golotsutskov Russia
2012 London	Yang Hak-seon South Korea	Denis Ablyazin Russia	Igor Radivilov Ukraine
2016 Rio de Janeiro	Ri Se-gwang North Korea	Denis Ablyazin Russia	Kenzo Shirai Japan
2020 Tokyo	Shin Jea-hwan South Korea	Denis Ablyazin ROC	Artur Davtyan Armenia
2024 Paris	Carlos Yulo Philippines	Artur Davtyan Armenia	Harry Hepworth Great Britain

Trampoline, Individual

Games	Gold	Silver	Bronze
2000 Sydney	Alexander Moskalenko Russia	Ji Wallace Australia	Mathieu Turgeon Canada
2004 Athens	Yuri Nikitin Ukraine	Alexander Moskalenko Russia	Henrik Stehlik Germany
2008 Beijing	Lu Chunlong China	Jason Burnett Canada	Dong Dong China
2012 London	Dong Dong China	Dmitry Ushakov Russia	Lu Chunlong China
2016 Rio de Janeiro	Uladzislau Hancharou Belarus	Dong Dong China	Gao Lei China
2020 Tokyo	Ivan Litvinovich Belarus	Dong Dong China	Dylan Schmidt New Zealand
2024 Paris	Ivan Litvinovich Individual Neutral Athletes	Wang Zisai China	Yan Langyu China

WOMEN

All-around, individual

Games	Gold	Silver	Bronze
2000 Sydney	Simona Amânar Romania	Maria Olaru Romania	Liu Xuan China
2004 Athens	Carly Patterson United States	Svetlana Khorkina Russia	Zhang Nan China
2008 Beijing	Nastia Liukin United States	Shawn Johnson United States	Yang Yilin China

Games	Gold	Silver	Bronze
2012 London	Gabby Douglas United States	Viktoria Komova Russia	Aliya Mustafina Russia
2016 Rio de Janeiro	Simone Biles United States	Aly Raisman United States	Aliya Mustafina Russia
2020 Tokyo	Sunisa Lee United States	Rebeca Andrade Brazil	Angelina Melnikova ROC
2024 Paris	Simone Biles United States	Rebeca Andrade Brazil	Sunisa Lee United States

All-around, teams

Games	Gold	Silver	Bronze
2000 Sydney	Romania(ROU) Simona Amânar Loredana Boboc Andreea Isărescu Maria Olaru Claudia Presăcan Andreea Răducan	Russia(RUS) Anna Chepeleva Anastasiya Kolesnikova Svetlana Khorkina Yekaterina Lobaznyuk Yelena Produnova Elena Zamolodchikova	United States (USA)[1] Amy Chow Jamie Dantzscher Dominique Dawes Kristen Maloney Elise Ray Tasha Schwikert

Games	Gold	Silver	Bronze
2004 Athens	Romania(ROU) Oana Ban Alexandra Eremia Cătălina Ponor Monica Roșu Nicoleta Daniela Șofronie Silvia Stroescu	United States (USA) Mohini Bhardwaj Annia Hatch Terin Humphrey Courtney Kupets Courtney McCool Carly Patterson	Russia (RUS) Ludmila Ezhova Svetlana Khorkina Maria Kryuchkova Anna Pavlova Elena Zamolodchikova Natalia Ziganshina
2008 Beijing	China (CHN) Cheng Fei Deng Linlin He Kexin Jiang Yuyuan Li Shanshan Yang Yilin	United States (USA) Shawn Johnson Nastia Liukin Chellsie Memmel Samantha Peszek Alicia Sacramone Bridget Sloan	Romania(ROU) Andreea Acatrinei Gabriela Drăgoi Andreea Grigore Sandra Izbașa Steliana Nistor Anamaria Tămârjan
2012 London	United States (USA) Gabby Douglas McKayla Maroney Aly Raisman Kyla Ross Jordyn Wieber	Russia(RUS) Ksenia Afanasyeva Anastasia Grishina Viktoria Komova Aliya Mustafina Maria Paseka	Romania (ROU) Diana Bulimar Diana Chelaru Larisa Iordache Sandra Izbașa Cătălina Ponor

Games	Gold	Silver	Bronze
2016 Rio de Janeiro	United States (USA) Simone Biles Gabby Douglas Laurie Hernandez Madison Kocian Aly Raisman	Russia(RUS) Angelina Melnikova Aliya Mustafina Maria Paseka Daria Spiridonova Seda Tutkhalyan	China(CHN) Fan Yilin Mao Yi Shang Chunsong Tan Jiaxin Wang Yan
2020 Tokyo	ROC (ROC) Lilia Akhaimova Viktoria Listunova Angelina Melnikova Vladislava Urazova	United States (USA) Simone Biles Jordan Chiles Sunisa Lee Grace McCallum	Great Britain (GBR) Jennifer Gadirova Jessica Gadirova Alice Kinsella Amelie Morgan
2024 Paris	United States (USA) Simone Biles Jade Carey Jordan Chiles Sunisa Lee Hezly Rivera	Italy (ITA) Angela Andreoli Alice D'Amato Manila Esposito Elisa Iorio Giorgia Villa	Brazil (BRA) Rebeca Andrade Jade Barbosa Lorrane Oliveira Flávia Saraiva Júlia Soares

Balance Beam

Games	Gold	Silver	Bronze
2000 Sydney	Liu Xuan China	Yekaterina Lobaznyuk Russia	Yelena Produnova Russia
2004 Athens	Cătălina Ponor Romania	Carly Patterson United States	Alexandra Eremia Romania
2008 Beijing	Shawn Johnson United States	Nastia Liukin United States	Cheng Fei China

Games	Gold	Silver	Bronze
2012 London	Deng Linlin China	Sui Lu China	Aly Raisman United States
2016 Rio de Janeiro	Sanne Wevers Netherlands	Laurie Hernandez United States	Simone Biles United States
2020 Tokyo	Guan Chenchen China	Tang Xijing China	Simone Biles United States
2024 Paris	Alice D'Amato Italy	Zhou Yaqin China	Manila Esposito Italy

Floor Exercise

Games	Gold	Silver	Bronze
2000 Sydney	Elena Zamolodchikova Russia	Svetlana Khorkina Russia	Simona Amânar Romania
2004 Athens	Cătălina Ponor Romania	Nicoleta Daniela Șofronie Romania	Patricia Moreno Spain
2008 Beijing	Sandra Izbașa Romania	Shawn Johnson United States	Nastia Liukin United States
2012 London	Aly Raisman United States	Cătălina Ponor Romania	Aliya Mustafina Russia
2016 Rio de Janeiro	Simone Biles United States	Aly Raisman United States	Amy Tinkler Great Britain
2020 Tokyo	Jade Carey United States	Vanessa Ferrari Italy	Angelina Melnikova ROC Mai Murakami Japan

2024 Paris	Rebeca Andrade Brazil	Simone Biles United States	Ana Bărbosu Romania

Floor Exercise

Games	Gold	Silver	Bronze
2000 Sydney	Svetlana Khorkina Russia	Ling Jie China	Yang Yun China
2004 Athens	Émilie Le Pennec France	Terin Humphrey United States	Courtney Kupets United States
2008 Beijing	He Kexin China	Nastia Liukin United States	Yang Yilin China
2012 London	Aliya Mustafina Russia	He Kexin China	Beth Tweddle Great Britain
2016 Rio de Janeiro	Aliya Mustafina Russia	Madison Kocian United States	Sophie Scheder Germany
2020 Tokyo	Nina Derwael Belgium	Anastasia Ilyankova ROC	Sunisa Lee United States
2024 Paris	Kaylia Nemour Algeria	Qiu Qiyuan China	Sunisa Lee United States

Vault

Games	Gold	Silver	Bronze
2000 Sydney	Elena Zamolodchikova Russia	Andreea Răducan Romania	Yekaterina Lobaznyuk Russia
2004 Athens	Monica Roșu Romania	Annia Hatch United States	Anna Pavlova Russia

Games	Gold	Silver	Bronze
2008 Beijing	Hong Un-jong North Korea	Oksana Chusovitina Germany	Cheng Fei China
2012 London	Sandra Izbașa Romania	McKayla Maroney United States	Maria Paseka Russia
2016 Rio de Janeiro	Simone Biles United States	Maria Paseka Russia	Giulia Steingruber Switzerland
2020 Tokyo	Rebeca Andrade Brazil	MyKayla Skinner United States	Yeo Seo-jeong South Korea
2024 Paris	Simone Biles United States	Rebeca Andrade Brazil	Jade Carey United States

Rhythmic gymnastics - All-around, individual

Games	Gold	Silver	Bronze
2000 Sydney	Yulia Barsukova Russia	Yulia Raskina Belarus	Alina Kabaeva Russia
2004 Athens	Alina Kabaeva Russia	Irina Tchachina Russia	Anna Bessonova Ukraine
2008 Beijing	Evgeniya Kanaeva Russia	Inna Zhukova Belarus	Anna Bessonova Ukraine
2012 London	Evgeniya Kanaeva Russia	Darya Dmitriyeva Russia	Liubov Charkashyna Belarus
2016 Rio de Janeiro	Margarita Mamun Russia	Yana Kudryavtseva Russia	Ganna Rizatdinova Ukraine
2020 Tokyo	Linoy Ashram Israel	Dina Averina ROC	Alina Harnasko Belarus

2024 Paris	Darja Varfolomeev Germany	Boryana Kaleyn Bulgaria	Sofia Raffaeli Italy

Rhythmic gymnastics - All-around, group

Games	Gold	Silver	Bronze
2000 Sydney	Russia (RUS) Irina Belova Natalia Lavrova Mariya Netesova Yelena Shalamova Vera Shimanskaya Irina Zilber	Belarus(BLR) Tatyana Ananko Tatyana Belan Anna Glazkova Irina Ilyenkova Maria Lazuk Olga Puzhevich	Greece(GRE) Eirini Aindili Evangelia Christodoulou Maria Georgatou Zacharoula Karyami Charikleia Pantazi Anna Pollatou
2004 Athens	Russia (RUS) Olesya Belugina Olga Glatskikh Tatiana Kurbakova Natalia Lavrova Elena Murzina Yelena Posevina	Italy (ITA) Elisa Blanchi Fabrizia D'Ottavio Marinella Falca Daniela Masseroni Elisa Santoni Laura Vernizzi	Bulgaria(BUL) Eleonora Kezhova Zhaneta Ilieva Zornitsa Marinova Kristina Rangelova Galina Tancheva Vladislava Tancheva
2008 Beijing	Russia (RUS) Margarita Aliychuk Anna Gavrilenko Tatiana Gorbunova Yelena Posevina Daria Shkurikhina Natalia Zuyeva	China(CHN) Cai Tongtong Chou Tao Lü Yuanyang Sui Jianshuang Sun Dan Zhang Shuo	Belarus(BLR) Olesya Babushkina Anastasia Ivankova Zinaida Lunina Glafira Martinovich Ksenia Sankovich Alina Tumilovich

Games	Gold	Silver	Bronze
2012 London	Russia (RUS) Anastasia Bliznyuk Uliana Donskova Ksenia Dudkina Alina Makarenko Anastasia Nazarenko Karolina Sevastyanova	Belarus(BLR) Maryna Hancharova Anastasia Ivankova Nataliya Leshchyk Aliaksandra Narkevich Ksenia Sankovich Alina Tumilovich	Italy (ITA) Elisa Blanchi Romina Laurito Marta Pagnini Elisa Santoni Anzhelika Savrayuk Andreea Stefanescu
2016 Rio de Janeiro	Russia (RUS) Vera Biryukova Anastasia Bliznyuk Anastasia Maksimova Anastasia Tatareva Maria Tolkacheva	Spain (ESP) Sandra Aguilar Artemi Gavezou Elena López Lourdes Mohedano Alejandra Quereda	Bulgaria(BUL) Reneta Kamberova Lyubomira Kazanova Mihaela Maevska-Velichkova Tsvetelina Naydenova Hristiana Todorova
2020 Tokyo	Bulgaria (BUL) Simona Dyankova Stefani Kiryakova Madlen Radukanova Laura Traets Erika Zafirova	ROC(ROC) Anastasia Bliznyuk Anastasia Maksimova Angelina Shkatova Anastasia Tatareva Alisa Tishchenko	Italy (ITA) Martina Centofanti Agnese Duranti Alessia Maurelli Daniela Mogurean Martina Santandrea

Games	Gold	Silver	Bronze
2024 Paris	China (CHN) Guo Qiqi Hao Ting Huang Zhangjiayang Wang Lanjing Ding Xinyi	Israel (ISR) Ofir Shaham Diana Svertsov Adar Friedmann Romi Paritzki Shani Bakanov	Italy (ITA) Alessia Maurelli Martina Centofanti Agnese Duranti Daniela Mogurean Laura Paris

Trampoline, Individual

Games	Gold	Silver	Bronze
2000 Sydney	Irina Karavayeva Russia	Oxana Tsyhuleva Ukraine	Karen Cockburn Canada
2004 Athens	Anna Dogonadze Germany	Karen Cockburn Canada	Huang Shanshan China
2008 Beijing	He Wenna China	Karen Cockburn Canada	Ekaterina Khilko Uzbekistan
2012 London	Rosannagh MacLennan Canada	Huang Shanshan China	He Wenna China
2016 Rio de Janeiro	Rosannagh MacLennan Canada	Bryony Page Great Britain	Li Dan China
2020 Tokyo	Zhu Xueying China	Liu Lingling China	Bryony Page Great Britain
2024 Paris	Bryony Page Great Britain	Viyaleta Bardzilouskaya Individual Neutral Athletes	Sophiane Méthot Canada